WINTER SPRING SUMMER FALL

living and lasting in missions

D1024178

ryan j. murphy

FATHER'S PRESS

To contact Ryan Murphy:
Email—rhmurphy@aimint.net
Blog—strangersinkenya.blogspot.com
Podcast—allthatyoucant.blogspot.com
Web page—murphy.kijabe.org

Cover photo: Chris Murphy
Cover design: Jessica Garcia and Heather Murphy

First printing, April 2010

Printed in the United States.

ISBN 978-0-9825321-2-6

Father's Press, LLC

Lee's Summit, MO
(816) 600-6288
www.fatherspress.com
Email—fatherspress@yahoo.com

Table of Contents

ACKNOWLEDGEMENTS

Thanks to…

Heather, my wife and perfect partner in this life of "leaving it all behind." You always make me smile in this life, and I can't wait to hang out with you in Heaven.

Our family, friends, and churches in America. We cherish every ounce of abundant support you give us.

Cindy Strobeck and Suzanne Geba, my trusty editors. Your encouragement through life and through ink is priceless.

Jessica Garcia . Thanks for your design and layout. Tech geeks are so chic.

The Philly Murphs—Chris, Kim, Maddy, Jack, and Alex. Thanks for the photo shoot at dawn.

Shaun Farrell of Singularity Audio, producer of my podcast *All That You Can't Leave Behind.* You were the spark that ignited this book.

Songwriter James Taylor ("You've got a friend") and poet e. e. cummings ("anyone lived in a pretty how town") for title inspiration.

Mike Smitley and Father's Press. You are touching the world through the pages you print.

You, the reader. You are taking my two books and passing them around your circles. Keep doing everything you can to share God's love for the poor and unreached of the world.

INTRODUCTION

It's September as I type. Technically still summer, the Pennsylvania weather is struggling not to succumb to autumn too early. Every few days, we'll get a stretch of still air and intense sun, but cool breezes and cloud cover are the new norm. A few leaves have already surrendered. Sometimes the chilly air knocks them off their branches, and the lush, green grass of summer gains the decorations of fall. Local wisdom says that "Indian summer" will still have its say, transporting us back to the blistering heat and humidity of early August. But today it's cool. Feels like fall. And the beauty and uniqueness of the next season of the year have us all longing for the change.

Thirteen years have passed for me since I've been a part of this transition. I traded the blessed predictability of long cold winters and relentlessly hot summers for the ho-hum monotony of sunny, cool days 365 days a year as a sophomore in college. I thought I had inhabited a different planet when it refused to rain for my first seven months in San Diego, California. Eventually, some rain did come, and I learned about a season I'd never experienced on the East Coast—the rainy season. San Diegans had come to expect long, long stretches without much precipitation but knew that winter would bring some rains. Not enough rain to sustain a region with millions of inhabitants (they'd need pipes from the Colorado River for that) but some rain, nevertheless.

Of course, San Diego still went through the motions of the seasons like the rest of the United States—winter, spring, summer, and fall—but the weather lacked the severity of most places. I remember surfing and sun bathing on a nice day in mid-December (not the norm) and wearing jeans and long sleeves in July (not the norm either) in Southern California. While California natives may be quick to brag about their luxurious climate, I found they still had a secret longing for real seasons. My clues? Beanies on heads when the weather dipped below 60, mass pilgrimages east to the foliage of the mountains in October, and inflatable light-up snowmen at Christmas time.

There seems to be something innate in us that enjoys the cyclical nature of living on earth. We find comfort in predictability. We enjoy celebrating birthdays and anniversaries and holidays, over and over again. We love the consistency of it all. The writer of Ecclesiastes says, "For everything there is a season," and this seems to be true—in the emotional, physical, and spiritual realm, on the community and national level, and concerning the weather patterns of this orb where we exist.

The people who initially experience these seasons with us are our families. We are born and raised in some kind of a family unit that teaches us how to act at funerals, where to sit at Halloween parades, and what a red sky at night will bring the next day. We accept a few others into this circle—neighbors, church members, teachers, friends—but these are the people who will teach us culture. But not all at once. It takes years. It takes seasons.

Over time, we learn how to physically survive and then how to learn. Next, we need to figure out how to socially stay afloat; puberty and adolescence act as our harsh drill sergeants for this. Contributing to and participating in society comes next, and it's usually college or trade school that paves the way over that hurdle. And the last thing that makes us human? Find a mate and procreate. From there, the cycle repeats.

Through all of this learning and living, something else huge is going on. Values are passed down. Beliefs are taught. Worldview is established. None of this happens in a day or in one place. It's woven into the fabric of everything we've ever done and everything we've ever experienced. It's taken many, many seasons of learning before any person can utter "I believe this" or "I know this to be true."

I went through one cultural change when I was 19. I remember sitting on a trolley where I was the only white face anywhere. That had never happened to me before. I remember trying guacamole for the first time, perhaps the greatest day of my life. (Don't tell my wife.) I remember standing in a kitchen smiling like an idiot as everyone around me conversed in

Spanish, probably laughing at the funny *gringo*. To an extent, I had to learn how to live all over again when I moved those 3,000 miles.

After nine years though, and a significant amount of seasons, I could comfortably call San Diego home. I figured out how not to get killed on the freeways. I found friends and a church to enrich my life. I learned to recognize all the Spanish cuss words to keep those embarrassing moments at bay. I gained experience in relating to those whose skin tone was a different shade of brown than mine. All of these things didn't happen overnight. They didn't happen in a few weeks. It took seasons to make friends, to help others, to make lasting contributions to society, and ultimately to become a part of San Diego.

Adjusting to new cultures takes time, whether you're moving down the street or flying across the continent. That's because hundreds of sub-cultures exist within America—the great melting pot. However, there are traits that still make America, America. San Diego had many differences from my Pennsylvania home, but it was still the United States. I may have needed to start over when I transplanted in SoCal, but I certainly wasn't starting from scratch.

As America itself becomes more and more cross-cultural, its citizens are also changing. An amazing trend has emerged; people actually care. Millions are tired of self-centered, me-focused living and desire to help those in need. That desire is translating into a great wave of volunteerism within the U.S. and charitable contributions towards the poor. Within the American church, this has manifested itself in a boom of mission trips to Third World countries as close as Mexico and the Dominican Republic and as far away as Russia and China.

Short-term trips, usually lasting around eleven days each, offer excellent opportunities to open the eyes of Americans to the realities of life outside our borders. They experience new customs and climates, hear new languages, and taste new foods. Often, short-termers will return home changed people, resolved to live and believe differently than they did before the trip.

Most short-term trips produce some sort of tangible result from their stay—a church or a well or a house—that blesses some poor individual or group. Many Americans will cherish an opportunity to visit with widows and orphans or perhaps speak with native believers. These relational contacts often prove to be the most memorable part of the trips for the visitors.

However, for all of the positive things that come from short-term missions trips, the one thing they can never produce is seasons. No matter how much you pray about your trip and how blessed your conversations are, you can't generate years of relationship in two weeks. Seasons require time. And it's within seasons that relationships grow, culture is learned, and the lasting fruit of evangelism blossoms.

My intention is not to belittle short-term missions; there are many wonderful benefits to them. When short-term mission trips are done right, they can be an enormous blessing to those who are visited and who are making the trip. I myself went on a short-term trip during college that forever changed my future. There is a place for short-term missions.[1]

My goal is to speak honestly about career missions. My first book, *All That You Can't Leave Behind*, chronicled my rookie year as a career missionary, and I didn't pull any punches. I wrote about loneliness, depression, and anger, but I also told stories of God's faithfulness, supernatural peace, and

---

[1] It also should be noted that there are so many different kinds of short-term missions done worldwide that it's hard to categorize them all together. I hope that some of my thoughts here might help guide readers towards embracing the most effective kinds of short-term trips.

profound inner joy. I told about bad haircuts, bad food, and bad health, but I balanced that with good friends, good experiences, and good chances to share Christ's love. All told, the missionary life is worth it because God and His glory are worth it. And I feel that is still true, now more than ever, after four years on the mission field.

As a career missionary, I've been able to see how those first year growing pains have produced long-term growth in me and in the relationships I've cultivated in Africa. If my cross-cultural experience had ended earlier, so would my growth. It's in relationships that true evangelism takes place, and my relationships grow with every passing season. My specific work may be different than that of another career missionary, but our shared goal—God's glory to the ends of the earth—blossoms with each day I spend in this cross-cultural environment.

Some would point to Paul—the writer of most of the New Testament—and his missionary journeys as a template against long-term missions, citing that he never spent decades in one place of ministry. Ironically though, Paul is the very definition of a career missionary. First of all, Paul didn't die in Tarsus or Jerusalem; he died where he spent his post-conversion life—on the mission field. That in itself shows that Paul's entire existence was about the Great Commission: "Go and make disciples of all nations" (Matthew 28:19).

Secondly, his desire was always to go where the Gospel had never been preached (2 Corinthians 5:15-16), but he didn't consider the job done until a church had been established. He would train leaders for months (sometimes years) and be a part of the people's lives. He would also have follow-up visits and letters to nurture the church and to strengthen the relationships he began. Paul didn't establish a healthy, self-sufficient church in two weeks.

Thirdly, Paul didn't need to spend twenty years in a city to build a church. If he did, he would have. Some use this fact to minimize the importance of career missionaries. But Paul shared a language (Greek), a government (Roman), and a religion (he usually went to the synagogues first) with his hearers. In other words, he had a lot of cultural common ground with his first converts. You could compare his cross-cultural transitions with mine in moving to San Diego from Pennsylvania. More similarities than differences awaited him in each city.

Lastly, Paul's heart was forever connected with the people along his journey. His prayers and letters testify to the depth of relationships formed by Paul.[2]

I could continue to define Paul as a quintessential career missionary, but I feel entirely confident in saying that Paul, our main model for "ends of the earth" evangelism in the Bible, more resembles a long-term missions man than a short-termer. He went through seasons of life with each group of people—the Corinthians, the Galatians, the Ephesians, the Philippians, and more—and built relational foundations that made his apostolic work astounding.

While my first cultural transition happened during my teen years, my second came as a 27-year-old with a wife and baby. After years of prayer and preparation, we found ourselves called to teach the children of missionaries in Kenya. Everyone who had visited or lived at the school where we were headed all gushed about one thing—the view. Nestled on the escarpment above the Great Rift Valley, the school has a 180-degree view of the brown or green valley (depending on the season) and the few mountains off in the distance. The closest one, a dormant volcano called Mt. Longonot, sits in the direction of our largest

---

[2] See 1 Thessalonians 3:7-10, 2 Corinthians 2:4, and Philippians 1:8 for Paul's words of affection for his churches.

sports field (rugby and soccer are the primary outdoor sports) and is also the biggest peak in our area.

However, when we arrived in July of 2005, no view awaited me. In fact, the valley could have been filled with pink dinosaurs and lollipop trees for all I knew. A thick fog sat on our hillside for the first weeks of our sojourn and made us feel like we were stranded on a cloud island in the sky rather than a school overlooking a gorgeous valley.

Residents of the school welcomed us warmly despite the chilly temperatures, which also came as a surprise for us newcomers. We left sweltering American summers and arrived to a chilly Southern Hemisphere winter. Not all places in Africa (or even Kenya, for that matter) see temperatures dip below 50 in June, July, and August, but with Rift Valley Academy seated at an elevation of 7,000 feet, we have a cold winter.

I keep using the term "winter" because my Western readers will get it. But winter is actually a foreign concept in sub-Saharan Africa. The normal dividing lines here aren't four—winter, spring, summer, and fall—but two. The dry season and the rainy season.

Corresponding to the precipitation is the temperature. The dry season happens when the region receives more direct sunlight (what we'd call summer); the rainy season happens when the region gets less direct sunlight (or winter, in our terminology). With the direct sunlight comes hotter temperatures, and without it comes cooler times. There are other nuances to the two basic seasons here (the short rains and the long rains, for example), but traditionally, there are just two seasons.

By my description above, you can tell which season we arrived in—the rainy season. The beautiful view became a running joke among the arriving staff, and we were dumbfounded to be making fires for warmth at 1 o'clock in the afternoon in early August. From day one in Africa, our normal understanding of seasons was flipped on its head.

While our school may be situated in a temperate locale, I feel it's important to mention that most missionaries worldwide have much more difficult climate adjustments to make. Throwing on a sweatshirt and thick socks is pretty easy to handle. Stoking the fire a little hotter during "summer" isn't an unbearable burden. Many of our colleagues, however, experience a rainy season in the low 90's with high humidity, and a dry season that's a crispy 120 degrees. Try singing "Jingle Bells" when your skin feels as if it's melting off. Or imagine three straight months of rain during what you've normally called the summer vacation months. These kinds of seasons are the most difficult to take. My adjustments in Kenya pale in comparison to theirs.

The fog did eventually lift. For a while. The valley was breathtaking, and Mt. Longonot was majestic. Rainy season lingered a few more weeks, with daily mist, frequent downpours, and just minutes of sun at a time, until the students arrived. And then it was gone. Completely.

The rains ended, and the warm weather moved in. The hot breeze blew across the valley floor, and the absence of cloud cover permitted the sun to quickly burn up the lush grass on our campus. Dust and dirt soon caked everything. Dry season had come.

And our first dry season was a bad dry season. Nine months without rain. Livestock died for lack of vegetation. In certain areas, some people died—either directly or indirectly—from the lack of crops and milk from animals. We were crying out to God for relief from this particularly extreme year.

I remember one dusty walk across campus with a colleague named Todd. He told me how May and June would be so wet and swampy that his schedule for P.E. classes would be a wreck. He said that every afternoon the rains would arrive, almost like clockwork, and send his students and him running for cover. I couldn't believe it. My forehead was sweaty and my tongue dusty—and it had been for over a hundred days in a row—and he was casually telling me about mud and precipitation.

But he was right. The drought broke. The rainy season came. Everyone rejoiced and thanked God for the new life brought by the rains. The valley and the mountains disappeared in fog, just like they had the year before.

Seasons.

You can't understand a place until you've been there through seasons. And not necessarily just one cycle of seasons. For us, the next dry season wouldn't be so severe. Two years later, the rainy season would almost completely miss us. No two years are exactly alike. There may be patterns, and there may be limits on how hot or how dry or how snowy the seasons may be, but each season has its own charm and distinction.

Similarly, you can't understand a people until you've been with them through seasons. Where I grew up in Pennsylvania, there traditionally weren't a lot of outsiders. Most of the residents settled here in the late 1700's or early 1800's, and they stayed here. They raised their families, and their kids married other settlers' kids, and that was pretty much it for about 200 years. I remember how locals would always note the distinction when mentioning someone who was "not from around here." Maybe he was a city slicker from Baltimore, or maybe she simply moved from the next county over. Nevertheless, it was important for them to know who had been there for years and seasons of life and who had not.

When you're an American traveling to another country, you stand out. If it's not your skin color, then it's your accent. If it's not your accent, then it's your clothing. If it's not your clothing, then it's your demeanor. You're an outsider, a foreigner, someone "not from around here," no matter how you try to disguise it. In the same way that our American culture can pick out a foreigner and be slow to embrace her, indigenous cultures don't simply throw open their homes and their hearts because "here comes the wonderful Americans." To put it bluntly, there is no way to become something completely other than what you are.

Career missionaries learn culture. They learn language. They may borrow cuisine, dress, home construction techniques, and mannerisms. But no matter how hard they try, they'll never be native to the culture. They'll always be "other."

But that's not a death sentence. That doesn't prompt us to throw up our hands and abandon worldwide missions because we can't completely become integrated with the people to whom we're ministering. It's not over.

The one thing we have going for us is seasons. Over time, the outsider begins to become part of the family, part of the community, part of the fabric of life within the native culture. The camp song goes, "They'll know we are Christians by our love," and everybody knows it's harder to love for a day than it is an hour, harder to love a week than a day, and harder to love for years than a few weeks. If the love is shown for enough seasons, often the message is given a chance.

Take Roger and Sue, missionaries in Eastern Kenya. They've lived for over 20 years in one of the climates I mentioned earlier, 90 degrees in the rainy season and 120 during the dry season. As they've sweated and toiled to evangelize, provide medical aid, and dig wells for the Orma people, they've seen few converts and no church established.

But they've seen a lot of seasons. The people gave them "cursed" land, but were shocked to watch them prosper and be blessed by God for years, giving living testimony to the power of God over their spiritual world. The people watched Roger and Sue raise their children and saw them grow up bilingual within that culture. They became intertwined in each other's families, becoming uncles and aunts for dozens of Orma people. In turn, the missionary kids have many "relatives" among the natives. On a daily basis God's truth is being taught—in word and in deed—and one day, I'm convinced, His Word will flourish in this dry and desolate place. And when it does, God will get the glory, and the seasons Roger and Sue spent there will have been the vehicle to make it happen.

The joy of seasons, and all the blessings that our time overseas brings us, is passed down to our children as well. Every year at the school where we work, dozens of seniors set their eyes to a future date when they'll be finished with their college and training in their home countries and will be able to return somewhere to the mission field. They find the cross-cultural relationships on the mission field as rewarding and fulfilling as their same-cultural ones (sometimes even more so) and long to return to the seasons of missionary life before they even leave our campus. I teach alongside a handful of people who have realized that dream—graduates of our school who now support missionaries in Africa through their calling to Rift Valley Academy.

Seasons can make a place home, but they also can make people your home. My two-year-old son asks frequently about his *tata* (the local Kenyan word for aunt). Since we've been back in the United States on home assignment, he doesn't ask about his toys in Africa or his playhouse or his cat. He asks about the person he loves most in Kenya—his *tata* who takes care of him for a few hours while mom and dad are teaching. His nine seasons of life have taught him to love regardless of color or accent or culture. Those seasons have made the people of Kenya his home.

The feeling is reciprocated too. As you become more at home in a culture, that culture embraces you and allows you to make yourself at home. Within that embrace, they also give you permission to share your beliefs and your worldview. They even trust you enough to let you challenge theirs. And that is precisely where missions happen.

We find precedence for cross-cultural ministry in the Bible. Think of Joseph. Faithful to God even in the worst of circumstances, he works and serves diligently in a foreign kingdom for years. Eventually, he is so trusted that Pharoah gives him the power to enact a plan to save hundreds of thousands of Egyptians from famine and to give his own family—the chosen people of God—a rich, new start. To the whole kingdom, the one true God of the universe was proclaimed.

Think of Daniel. He adapts to the culture of his captors while never betraying his own faith. An advisor so trusted and respected that four kings sought his counsel, Daniel's life provoked a multitude of people to give praise to his God.

Think of Esther. Another Hebrew captive in a pagan kingdom, her beauty and character elevated her to the position of favored wife of King Xerxes. As queen, she gained enough respect to appear before the king uninvited. Her bold plea for the lives of her people group not only saved them but also caused people of other nationalities to become Jews.[3]

Think even of Paul. As mentioned earlier, Paul's bouncing around the Mediterranean sometimes is used as fodder against the need for seasons in our missionary work. Although Paul didn't have the drastic language or cultural barriers to cross that many long-term missionaries today have, he still found it important to spend months and often years with the people to whom he ministered. And the product of those seasons was a self-sustaining, fully-established, and fitfully-growing church.

Seasons of ministry don't ensure quality, and they don't ensure tangible results. There is no secret formula when it comes to sharing the Gospel. We're not selling Coca-Cola. But seasons do put us in position—like Joseph, Daniel, Esther, and Paul were in—to impact the hearts and worldviews of our host cultures. And that, more often than not, is the kindling for wildfires of the Holy Spirit spreading to the far corners of the earth.

---

[3] Esther 8:17

My hope for this book is that it will continue where my last one left off (which it does chronologically from 2006) but also show how the life in missions is about more than just transitions. With every new experience, my ability to relate and communicate and love with the nationals[4] multiplies. With seasons come deeper understanding of culture and worldview, and with that understanding comes a sacred vehicle for communicating the good news of Jesus Christ into the hearts of the unreached.

I've organized this book into twelve chapters, like the twelve months of the year. My wife and I have spent four years total in Africa. Since my first book covers the rookie year, this one will cover our last three. Those three years are broken up by the four seasons that Americans typically experience—winter, spring, summer, and fall. You will be reading about those twelve seasons of our life in Africa in the twelve chapters to follow.

Each chapter will have two parts—"Lessons for Lasting" and "Stories of Living." I hope you enjoy the various tales from Africa in my "Stories of Living" sections. I'll cover stressful topics like dealing with Third World governments, balancing family and ministry, surviving civil war, and grieving both base poverty and tragic death. But, I'll also cover the lighter side of missionary life by taking you inside a lion's dining room, an African movie theater, a girls' basketball team huddle, and a Kenyan delivery room. However, this book has more than just stories of living in Africa.

The other section you'll find in each chapter is called "Lessons for Lasting." These sections contain a key Bible verse and an application that I feel missionaries (or those interested in

---

[4] *Nationals* is the term I'll use for the people to whom missionaries are sent, not the terms *natives* or *indigenous peoples*.

missions) can learn from. I'm by no means an expert after just four years, but I feel that if we each share the things we've experienced, perhaps this will "spur one another on to good works" on the mission field for years and years to come.

The seasons I've experienced in Africa have blessed me immeasurably. They've given me greater cultural familiarity. They've allowed me to learn more about myself and God. They've provided me with hundreds of relationships. They've helped me make Africa a home away from home. Perhaps these seasons have even helped me to abandon the illusory concept of "home" here on earth that we humans so often cling to, while straining ahead towards the future in Heaven that I long for.

Greater still, my seasons in Africa are allowing me to be the most effective missionary I can be. And that's what God wants from each of us whom He has called to go.

Part One

Summer

Lessons for Lasting
Rewards

Mark 10:29-31.
"I tell you the truth," Jesus replied, "no one who has left home
or brothers or sisters or mother or father or children or fields for
me and the gospel will fail to receive a hundred times as much
in this present age (homes, brothers, sisters, mothers, children
and fields—and with them, persecutions) and in the age to
come, eternal life."

From time to time, I'll get emails from former students
or youth group members—some of whom have now graduated
from college, I interject with an old man sigh—mentioning that
they are "interested" in missions. I tell them, "That's great!" but
I can't get much further into the conversation without
mentioning that "interest" in missions won't even get you off
the couch, let alone out your front door. I usually have two
simple pieces of advice for those who are at the starting point of
"interest" in missions.

One. Tell people. Tell your best friend. Tell your uncle.
Tell your church's mission pastor. Tell the guy who slices your
deli cheese. Tell the lady who cuts your hair. Why? Well, if
you're really truly sincerely interested, then you won't mind
other people knowing. If your interest is ever going to lead
somewhere realistically, then it's good for the key people in
your life to know ASAP. You may think this decision will only
affect you, but as soon as you pipe up with such an outlandish
idea, you'll find a chorus of voices who have a vested interest in
what you're planning—namely your parents and close relatives.

If you're serious about this, your loved ones deserve as much advance notice as you can possibly give.

But…if you're fearing the sacrifice or knowing that it's not probable for you or if you're afraid of what your family might think or if you're puffing yourself up as spiritual, you *won't* tell people. Because you really aren't interested.

The other benefit to telling people is that they will keep you accountable. They will encourage you down the road and help you take steps to reach your goal. Or perhaps they'll help you to see why you shouldn't actually go. In spring of 2004, our missions pastor had eight of us stand in front of the congregation, all of us claiming to be "interested" in missions. From there, conversations happened for many of us that led us closer or farther away from missions. Even though a few of those eight people haven't gone out (yet), they still are being helped and challenged toward the serious calling of career missions. "Interest" isn't enough. You need to tell people.

My other piece of advice on moving from "interested" to the mission field—know without a shadow of a doubt that there are huge rewards in mission work.

Sadly, the first thing that pops into the head when the word "missions" is uttered is sacrifice and struggle and loss. Those are certainly a part of the calling to missions, but the rewards dwarf the hardships. Paul wrote to the Corinthians that "our light and momentary troubles are achieving for us an eternal weight of glory that far outweighs them all." Our focus as believers in general and as missionaries in particular must be on the eternal glory, the rewards in store for us. Sure, you probably will see tangible fruit in your missions endeavor. Perhaps a Bible will be translated, a village will be converted, a deathbed patient saved, a child's life changed. Most likely there will be awesome rewards along the way for the missionary, but there's also a slight possibility that when you hold up the joys of the missionary life with the sacrifices—family, friends, comfort, cultural familiarity—you may not feel that they're even worth it. But you'll need to remember that there is a far greater reward than the singular joys of missionary life.

The verses that I need to come back to over and over are Jesus' words in Mark 10:29-31. "No one who has left [everything] for me and the gospel will fail to receive a hundred times as much in this present age and in the age to come, eternal life."

The leaving is necessary, but so is an expectation of reward.

I even take this verse one step further. For every missionary that goes out, dozens of family members and hundreds of friends are left behind. What's in it for them? What's their motivation to bestow a blessing on those departing? Again, I point to this verse.

For our last Christmas stateside in 2004, we were lucky enough to have all of our parents and siblings together for the holidays in San Diego. Although family gatherings aren't really the normal venue for elaborate speeches, I wanted to share this verse with everyone. I wanted to tell them about the blessings they could expect as they reluctantly and sadly but *willingly* allowed us to follow God's call to Africa. I don't think Mark 10:29-31 is just for those of us who go; I think it's for anyone and everyone who has given and sacrificed and lost big time for God's glory to go to the ends of the earth. Parents and friends included.

None of us—missionaries, parents of missionaries, relatives of missionaries, and friends of missionaries—can lose sight of those important points. We're not sacrificing for naught when we sign on to missions, and we will be rewarded for anything we've given up here on earth beyond what we could ever possibly imagine or expect.

Those are truths that I hope will get you to the mission field if you're "interested" and keep you there if you've gone.

Stories of Living

The stories from this season touch on families. First off, I discuss the crisis of African families, and then secondly the dilemma of Korean missionary families. Lastly, I share "Additions and Subtractions" to give some perspective on how many families come and go on a regular basis from our field.

Those without fathers

I went to my first orphanage on Saturday. A bus full of students drove down into the valley to a new one they've started called Little Lambs. We had a full day of projects ahead of us—planting two dozens trees around the property line, building a new barbed wire fence by the road, and painting the inside and outside of the kitchen/cafeteria.

The valley floor, although only five or six miles below our school, was a sauna—no wind, no shade, and a scorching sun. It was hot, dry, and dusty work, but the students served without grumbling. I mostly dug holes for the trees, dubiously wondering about their future as the hard clay gobbled up every last drop of water we gave to our arbor infants.

This orphanage is one of many "Little Lambs" orphanages that were originally begun by Africa Inland Mission missionaries and have now morphed into a strange hybrid of national/missionary leadership.

I'm not privy to all of the details, but our agency is scaling back their involvement with orphanages, seeing them as a political and financial negative and as an ineffective long-term salve for this gaping African wound. The orphanages that the agency is still partnering with are not traditional boarding orphanages. They are day orphanages.

Orphans obviously exist throughout the world, but the AIDS mess has created an orphan crisis here. Traditionally, orphans are taken in by their families. But when so many mothers and father are dying, the families become so large that they can't afford all of the children. Sometimes they'll kick children out; sometimes they just won't take them in to begin with.

Take Kamau for example. Kamau is a Christian man here in Kijabe, probably in his fifties. Walking is a laborious task for him as his one leg is crippled. Nevertheless, every Tuesday and Saturday you'll see him walking all over campus delivering eggs and flowers. If you saw the regular business he does on those two days alone, you'd think he was a fairly wealthy Kenyan man.

Tragically, two of Kamau's children (and their respective spouses) have died from AIDS in the past few years. Kamau has taken in all six of his orphaned grandchildren to save them from the streets. To pay for all of their clothing, food, and high school education would be a huge financial burden for Kamau.

A day orphanage helps someone like Kamau. It's free day care for the younger children, free schooling for the older kids, and free meals throughout the day—all provided by loving, Christian staff. Kamau doesn't need to worry about the children's safety while he is working, plus he has some of his financial burden lifted.

Take away the day orphanage from someone like Kamau, and he probably wouldn't be able to care for all six children. Possibly he could find a regular orphanage to take them in, but there is a likelihood that some would turn to crime, drugs, and prostitution. By providing assistance to families through the day orphanages, Christian workers here hope to keep some kind of family structure intact.

Of course, day orphanages don't work in every situation. There are millions of orphans in Africa who have no living relatives or have no willing relatives, and we need to help them too. But where should the emphasis be? If you have a dollar, how should you split it? Day orphanages? Full orphanages? Feeding programs? What about AIDS relief? If you slow AIDS down, you slow the orphan rate down. You can see how awfully thin your dollar is stretched.

For now, day orphanages seem to be a wonderful middle ground. I'll work to make places like this work for my community. I am not creating a place for children to be discarded. I am not pouring money or time into raising children that should be raised by their own families, if at all possible. But I am going half way. I am helping African families that are being ravished by AIDS (or by tribal unrest or any other reason) stay together by sharing their load each and every day.

That's a hole worth digging. That's a dollar worth giving.

Little Korea

Rift Valley Academy possesses the nickname "Little America" because of the large number of Americans who work here (about 90% of the staff) and attend here (about 55% of the student body). The highest concentration of American citizens on Kenyan soil exists within our 100-acre campus, so the nickname is very apropos. The second largest nationality represented is South Korea. In the future, could our school's nickname morph to "Little Korea"?

Far behind any of the world leaders in population and land mass, South Korean Christians have perhaps the biggest vision and commitment to world missions. In fact, they rank second in the world (after the United States) in numbers of missionaries sent to foreign countries. This is shocking when you consider that South Korea is the 25th most populated country in the world and is doubly shocking when you consider that Christians comprise only 35% of South Korea's population. They are a vibrant minority that will not wait to become a majority to shoulder a majority of Christ's Great Commission to the nations!

For Koreans the mission's boom of the past 50 years for Koreans has presented problems though. For the parents to be in the mission field, the children need education. Many evangelistic people throughout history have neglected their children for the sake of reaching the lost; this fault is not limited to Koreans. Rather than adopt a missions infrastructure that would support the Korean families and their home culture (schools, pastoral care, etc.), many Koreans have borrowed the American one.

This has come at a great cost. Most Korean parents acknowledge when they bring their child to "Little America" that, in time, their child will become a little American. The child will spend 75% of his/her year with American friends, mentors, and teachers. Many Korean students from RVA are then bound for American universities, where the process of becoming non-Korean will become complete.

The current predicament could be a case of the cart getting in front of the horse—the passion and fervor for the lost outrunning the consideration for the family. Westerners did the same thing when cross-cultural missions boomed at the turn of the 19th century—husbands and wives separating for years at a time, strangers raising children in home countries while parents lived and evangelized abroad—so there is no derisive finger pointing here. However, MK (missionary kid) care is now a well-established part of the American/Western infrastructure for missions, holding up the families healthily to fulfill their calling.

Our school is doing our best to help our "Little Korea" population. We have a full-time missionary couple on staff right now from South Korea. Jay and Ann act as translators between administration and staff and South Korean families, providing cultural insight and skilled communication for all involved. As parents themselves, they help South Korean kids relate to their missionary parents who are far away. As a part of the American school community, they help South Korean parents understand the cultural nuances that surround the children day-to-day. They could probably use a dozen more folks to help them in their roles as go-betweens, but Jay and Ann are working incredibly hard and remarkably efficiently on behalf of our South Korean constituency.

The hope is that South Koreans will build their own schools, catching a vision for the preservation of their own native culture and their children's place in it, and that hope may someday be realized. For now though, North American and South Korean missionaries are finding new ways to do missions that are healthily balanced for our Korean families. Our overarching desire is that we will be able to keep the pipeline of new cross-cultural missionaries from South Korea open and thriving for years to come. The fire for God that is sweeping through South Korea should be stoked in every way possible, and it's a good thing our school can be a part of that movement.

Additions and subtractions

It's the time of transitions at RVA right now. Graduation was last Saturday. Thirty-five of our 68 family units on campus will leave by next week (or have left already). Five new ones arrive tomorrow. Twenty more will arrive in mid-August. (Yes, you math experts, that does mean that we'll be understaffed this fall.)

With the exodus, we've had some additions to our family: a gray tabby cat that weighs more than a truck and a brown bunny named Chocolate. Micah also acquired a non-mammalian red, two-wheeler bike. Those are some of the fun parts to this transition phase.

The "unfun" parts are saying goodbye. Our goodbyes have had three varieties this time around. 1—People leaving RVA forever. They'll return to their homes around the world (mostly in the U.S. though) and chances are good we'll never see them on this side of eternity again. 2—People leaving RVA for a year. They plan on returning after a yearlong home assignment. 3—People leaving RVA for a few months. Some people are going on a short home assignment and plan on returning in January.

I probably have no analogy that would help you understand how large in scale this exodus is. But I'll try. Imagine your closest friends/acquaintances are the people who live in the 68 houses closest to you. Now, imagine half of them leaving in a two week span. Adios amigos.

I know we've all said goodbye, had friends move away, etc. so it's not like missionaries invented saying goodbye. But this scale we're dealing with is preposterous.

Hence, with 35 families leaving and 25 coming, it's felt like a carousel of flying furniture lately. But moving here at RVA has an added dimension to it. This will really confuse you, so hang on.

When people leave for good, they have to sell all of their things. Sometimes the people to whom they sell are on campus; sometimes they haven't arrived yet. Few of the sold items can be transferred until the people leave (which is what's happening now). So all at once, entire households worth of goods disappear into other households. However, those households are often in transition as well.

Once people move out of their houses, the school's maintenance team has to repair, repaint, and get them ready for the new residents coming in. The households for the people coming in are set up by "host families." So, the host families move furniture for the new families. Many of the people who are staying on campus (the host families) move as well. So, almost all families remaining on campus are moving at least one and sometimes two families within a two-week period.

But, the new households can't be set up until the old households are moved out. And sometimes people can't move out of the old houses until another house is fully prepared by maintenance. And sometimes old houses can't be moved out of until the occupants know where they are moving. With our staff still undecided for next year due to people still raising money to come out here, administration can't decide where everyone should be. Decisions on where to put each family are difficult because housing is very tight on campus; administration has to be careful to get the right person in the right spot. It's like dominoes and a jigsaw puzzle all rolled into one. And here I thought this phase of life would end after college. It turns out I might have another twenty or thirty years of this on the mission field.

This time around we're the lucky ones who don't have to move; we've been in the same house for six months straight now. But it's still a full-time job just getting other people in and out these days.

FALL

Lesson for Lasting
Communication

Romans 10:14-15
"How, then, can they call on the one they have not believed in? And how can they believe in the one of whom they have not heard? And how can they hear without someone preaching to them? And how can they preach unless they are sent? As it is written, "How beautiful are the feet of those who bring good news!""

Ask around your typical American church about missions, and you'll hear a common, yet proudly energetic phrase—*our church supports missionaries...*—which will then unfortunately be followed by—*...but I've never seen them.*

One of the reasons for this sad reality is the way that mainstream denominations in America have traditionally structured their international ministries. Many of them set up missions from the top, meaning that specific ministries and outreaches overseas are managed the way a member church in the States might be. If there is a financial need or a need for workers in any given area, the upper level church hierarchy will see that the need is met. If North Carolina needs a minister, the big guys on the national scene will find someone. If Brazil needs a new mission hospital, the American leaders will allocate funding to make it happen. For many denominational missionaries, going to the field is similar to applying for a new job. It certainly takes extraordinary faith to apply for any job in missions (I'm not downplaying their efforts at all), but in general, the denominational model tends to have some flaws

While their structure for missions may be efficient in a business sense, what is frequently lost is relationships. If I have applied for and procured a job, then I have an employer. I am responsible to that one person (or maybe a small board of people) for the work that I do; that person then is responsible for providing me with the support (financial, logistical, emotional, and in the case of missions, spiritual) to do my work. This structure for missions is very familiar to our capitalist culture.

In some cases, the denomination will set up tours for appearances by their missionaries when they have finished their assignments or are on home assignment. It's good for church members to know where a fraction of every offering plate dollar is going, and it does help them to have a face (even if it's just a fleeting face) to associate with the missions work of that church. After a few dozen churches are visited over a few dozen Sundays, that task of the denominational missionary is finished.

Overall, the relationships involved in this loop are few. The roles and duties of sender (employer) and missionary (employee) are clearly established. The congregations (the financiers) get occasional and brief reports. Like I said, it's an efficient model.

However, when it comes to worldwide missions, is efficiency really our highest goal?

Faith-based missions are the other main paradigm in practice today. Under this model, missionaries who are called to a specific work cannot go anywhere without people who know them and will stand behind them. These people will pray for them, test them, hold them accountable for the work, and pay for the work they are doing. I'll elaborate more on this structure, but for now, I want you to see how many quality relationships are required to make faith-based missions work.

If you're a part of a denominational church right now, chances are good that a minute portion of your weekly offering is going to some missionary somewhere. Did you know that? If so, do you know what kind of work that missionary does? If so, do you know the name of that missionary? And my last qualifier: if you do know the name of the missionary (or any missionary, for that matter) who is supported by your general church offering, have you ever met that person?

My guess is that most of your answers were no. In fact, if I had to make a wild bet, I'd guess that 99% of individuals in mainstream denominations have never met a missionary financially supported by his church's offering.

Relationships between the missionaries and their sending churches are a crucial component of world missions, and yet these relationships are so frequently neglected.

The faith-based missions paradigm has its relational flaws as well. Sometimes the missionaries are to blame. Sometimes they don't realize their responsibility to their supporters. They send infrequent emails and letters, they never schedule visits when they are home, and they don't maintain the friendships that they had before they left for the field.

Sometimes it's the fault of their financial circumstances. Some missionaries struggled so much to raise their support from so many people in so many locations that they are spread far and wide when they are home. To visit all of the different churches costs a lot of travel money, and if they do make it to all of their supporting areas, their visits are often very short.

Rather than drone on about the flaws of denominational and faith-based missions, I'd like to focus on a short but powerful verse. Romans 10:14-15 outlines the pecking order for the missionary movement. The beautiful, God-ordained plan actually starts earlier in the tenth chapter with the blueprint to salvation (confess with your mouth and believe in your heart that Jesus is Lord). From there, Paul wonders how they can confess and believe without hearing, how they can hear without a preacher, and how they can receive a preacher without one being sent to them. It's a pretty logical progression, and anyone with a basic understanding of evangelism and missions can grasp the concept.

However, I feel like the modern church has allowed the order of Paul's questions here to skew our prioritizing of the steps in missions. Since the "sending" part is last mentioned, it's as if it's least important. Our reading of this verse should lead us back the vine to the root rather than out from the vine to the intended fruit. Without the act of sending the missionaries, there is no way for anyone to be saved. It starts with sending.

If it all starts with sending, then that would make the senders of utmost importance, not necessarily the missionaries. It is the senders' vision, the senders' desire, and the senders' love for the lost that fuels missions.

Now, is that how most missions today are operating? Is the denominational model mentioned earlier the pattern? No. The senders (the average Christians sitting in a pew) have little connection to the work that is being done by the missionaries. The organization itself may have made it a priority, but that doesn't mean there is a healthy connection between missionary and church member.

In the faith-based model, do we see a "sender-driven" root for the missions work? Sometimes, but not always. In many cases, we will find healthy churches giving a balanced and biblical view on the Christian calling to reach all nations for Jesus. Out of that calling, individuals rise up and answer the call to go, which then is partially financed by the home church itself. Unfortunately, there are also some cases where the missionary answers the call only to find himself without a church that desires to send or understands its role in the missions endeavor. A missionary without a clear "home church" to send him out is likely to struggle greatly. And it's no wonder. These verses in Romans lay out the pattern for us perfectly. It starts with senders. Senders are the foundational part of missions.

If you are a sender reading this, thank you. The Gospel would not be reaching the ends of the earth without you. My only plea is that you realize the importance of your role in all of this. Don't stop praying and preaching about missions. Don't allow your church's focus to drift. Don't lose focus of why you are giving. Stay connected with your missionaries. Demand that they stay connected with you. Always see yourself as center, not as peripheral, to the wonderful work being accomplished around the globe.[1]

For my fellow missionaries reading this, I must restate the obvious—you don't exist without a sender. Without their financial support, without their prayer support, and without their sending vision, you don't exist. Sometimes after months and years on the mission field, the old "out of sight, out of mind" adage comes into play for missionaries. We forget where we came from and how we got here.

This cannot happen. We must never lose sight of the value of our sending churches and individuals or of our responsibility to them. We must always make room for those who have sent us out to minister to the poor and unreached. Whether it be through emails, cards, pictures, websites, blogs, personal visits and interactions during home assignments, or anything else—these relationships are vital to the success and length of your missionary work.[2]

May the sentence, "Our church supports missionaries, but I've never seen them," be replaced with, "I know, love, and partner with the missionaries our church supports!" because missionaries and senders work together seamlessly in the work of reaching the lost.

Stories of Living

One of the ways that I've stayed connected with my support team in the States is through my blog—*Strangers In Kenya*. I send monthly emails and periodic snail mail letters with the "big news" of our ministry. But for those who are very involved

---

[1] For more encouragement and ideas on your role in missions, I'd suggest *Serving as Senders* by Neal Pirolo.

[2] For more information on how to strengthen your connections with your support team, I recommend *Friend Raising* by Elizabeth Barrett.

with our work, I've written stories (many of which make up this book and my first) about faith, culture, and life. These three stories—"*LOST* Again," "Weather or not," and "See you at the movies"—focus on the cultural differences of an African city from an American one and adjusting to life in a new geographical climate.

LOST again

The season three debut of *LOST* was last night in the U.S., and ironically, my wife Heather and I finished watching season two on DVD after the boys went to bed. As soon as we finished a disc, we passed it along to the next series-addicted missionaries. I'm not even sure how long the waiting list is for the show right now, but it's substantial.

Although the show started when we were in the U.S. in 2004-2005, we never watched it. Then, our first few months here in Africa, Zac and Shelbi in San Diego sent us the whole first season on DVD, and the craze began. Soon after, the discs began making their rounds through campus—doctors, dorm parents, administration, Bible teachers were instantly hooked.

I know it's a huge hit everywhere, but some fellow missionaries and I have discussed why it seems to particularly resonate here in Kijabe, in Kenya, among missionaries. Try some of these on.

Forty-eight people land in a remote area where they've never before been. They have to learn how to survive physically, socially, and emotionally for an indefinite period of time. Their days are filled with uncertainty and heartache. They miss home. Every once in a while, their fellow survivors up and vanish. The Others, those who are unknown and different from them, are out there—possibly to bring danger, possibly to bring blessings. (And at RVA, since we're a boarding school responsible for the safety of 450+ children, we have a fence around campus, making us feel like we're on an island.) It's no wonder how sometimes, in some small ways, we feel like *LOST* is very much our story.

Although everyone on *LOST* wants to get off the island (except for the insecure mystic John Locke), not everyone here desires escape, so that's one key difference. We've chosen to be missionaries. Another difference is that we know why we're here (to see Jesus Christ praised in every corner of the earth); after two seasons, they still haven't told us what the heck the Dharma Initiative is. Supposedly it's important but we'll have to wait and see. Oh, and there are no polar bears, slave ships, or black, smoky, swirling forces of death in Kenya either. I forgot about those.

As we finished season two, it seemed like the 48 survivors were closer and closer to escape and rescue, and again, their situation felt eerily similar to ours. With the upcoming elections and political tensions, we as a school are discussing contingency plans for various scenarios. Any number of things could transpire at any time, and so we want to be ready. We had a meeting just yesterday going over a 40+ page plan to prepare us for anything.

So as we missionaries here escape the realities of our own tale of survival, we put ourselves in the shoes of the survivors (or are they all dead?) of Oceanic Flight 815. But we never wonder if we're lost. As 2 Corinthians 5 says, "We are pressed on every side, but not crushed; perplexed, but not in despair...For our light and momentary troubles are achieving for us an eternal glory that far outweighs them all." We are not lost, but we go on for those who are.

(Hit the gong and cue the blurry, slowly spinning *LOST* title.)

Weather or not

Your first year in a new location is basically a model. It's normal. It's what you've known. I remember moving to San Diego in May of 1996, and waking up every morning to ridiculously blue skies for eight months straight. I felt like Bill Murray in *Groundhog's Day*. It was the same day every day.

Well, last year the rainy season dried up in September and it was dry, hot, and sunny for about six months straight. That was my model for this place, but it turns out that last year was an anomaly. The dry season does come to Kenya, but usually not until after December starts. This year, I've been told, is much closer to the norm, and we've had rain, rain, rain.

Almost every day or night for the past three months we've had precipitation. It's been great. The shambas (gardens) of the locals are doing great, and even the valley is green right now. Last year it was brown from October to April. This year our wells are all sufficiently filled, and we haven't had water rationing during this entire term.

My faulty expectations have caught me unprepared more than a few times, however. We live right on the side of the mountain range and all of our weather comes from the other side of the mountain. So, if it's sunny and 80 in Kijabe and sunny and 80 in the valley, you think, "Great...short sleeves, no jacket." But then one cloud starts to peek over the ridge. And another. And another until the sky above you is totally black, all within the span of about 20 minutes. Pretty soon it's 60 degrees, rainy, and windy, and you are running from classroom to classroom for dear life.

That, however, is just one minor difference from last year to this one.

The most interesting change from last year to this is the increased wildlife. Because there is more rain, there is more vegetation. More vegetation means more bugs to eat the vegetation. More bugs means more predators, like birds and spiders. The birds here are beautiful overall, but a group of ibises have begun to terrorize our area with their raucous calls each dawn and dusk. Micah and I have thrown our share of rocks at those nuisances. As for the spiders, let's just say that I turn the light on when I go to the bathroom in the middle of the night now. A family of half dollar-sized critters have moved in, and every day we find one lurking in our *choo* (toilet). Lucky for us they aren't very speedy.

The most irksome new pest of this fall is popularly called Nairobi Eyes. This little guy looks like a hybrid between a ladybug and an ant. Its tail is red and its body black. It crawls in through cracks in the doors and windows at night, attracted by the light. Then, it'll fall from the ceiling on you. You feel something and brush it off with your hand. And when you touch it, its body gives off poison, which the fingertips and palms of your hands are immune to. But every body part you subsequently touch with those hands will be contaminated.

I haven't gotten the rash yet, but from what I hear, it's kind of like poison ivy that burns more. It goes away more quickly than poison ivy (around 24 hours), but if you scratch at it, then your fingertips will again carry the poison and spread it all over your body.

While we are so glad for the rain, we have sacrificed some sleep because of it. Not only is the sound of rain on metal roofing quite noisy, the fear of giant spiders crawling through our sheets or Nairobi Eyes dropping on us from the ceiling keeps us vigilant throughout the night. Rain for sleep—it's a fair trade.

See you at the movies

The lights go down, the audience quiets, and grainy footage of a Kenyan flag appears on the screen. Everyone in the movie theater stands for the playing of the Kenyan national anthem.

This is how the movie experience begins in a Third World country.

Nairobi is one of the largest cities in Africa, so it does offer certain cultural amenities, like movies. Every few months we'll spend a Saturday with students or fellow missionaries at one of the few movie theaters watching a fairly recent flick. We usually get movies a good month after their release dates, but before they are released to video in the States. Only blockbusters are released here simultaneously with their US release dates. Mike, a Bible teacher who lives three hours east of us, saw *Star Wars Episode III* 10 hours before his buddies in Texas, but like I said, it's only movies as big as that which will be debut here quickly.

The theaters are pretty nice. Good seats, large screens, adequate sound systems. The ticket prices aren't bad, comparatively speaking. About 5 dollars a flick. The popcorn and soda are cheap as well, but they don't sell the 5 liter cups and the trash basket-sized popcorns here. It's a reasonable size for human consumption, a novel idea that American theaters seemingly abandoned ages ago.

There are downfalls too. The machines break down a bit more here, and there are no refunds. You can go see another movie if you like or just wait all day for it to be fixed. There are only a few movies to choose from in the entire city, and quite a few of them are Indian films or native African films. And then there is the issue of a ratings system.

Ah, yes. There is no ratings system. At the bottom of every poster and every flier, at the beginning of every trailer and every movie, there is no rating to be found. No R, PG-13, PG…nothing.

In the States, I use those ratings for the iffy movies, you know, the ones that look funny or unique, but just might have too much offensive content to be worth their artistic value. They help me guard my heart from unnecessary evil. Yes, usually you can tell what kind of movie you're in for by the trailer or the synopsis or even the poster, but not always.

I'll give you an example of why I miss the ratings system. Last month I saw a movie trailer over the summer for a movie about a poor Third World man who travels to America to learn their culture. The trailer showed him meeting with government officials, learning American jokes from a comedy coach, and wandering starry-eyed through Times Square. I'm a cross-cultural missionary, and so insights into culture and the humorous side of cultural differences looked like a real winner to me. The preview reminded me of Belky from that 80's sitcom *Perfect Strangers*.

So, after school let out last term, a fellow teacher and I went to see the movie that I'd been raving about since I'd seen the clip over the summer. In short, two missionaries show up in the theater. After fifteen minutes, two missionaries leave the theater.

The movie was vile, lacked any redeeming value, and was certainly rated R in the States. The clips in the trailer must have been the only "clean" clips in that movie; nothing else that we saw in our fifteen minutes was.

If anything positive came out of that experience though, we did see a trailer for *The Nativity Story*, a movie about Mary and Joseph and Christmas. Hopefully that will be in theaters here in time to get us in the holiday spirit. Which holiday, you ask? Easter of course. And hopefully the shepherds aren't foul-mouthed and the Wise Men keep their clothes on. I'm hoping this one is rated something other than R, so I can actually watch the whole thing.

WINTER

Lessons for Lasting
Stress

Philippians 3:10-11.
"I want to know Christ and the power of his resurrection and the fellowship of sharing in his sufferings, becoming like him in his death, and so, somehow, to attain the resurrection from the dead."

I gave a Friday chapel talk during this season on the power of the resurrection. Friday chapels are unique at our school because the entire campus gathers around the flagpole to honor the Kenyan flag and to hear God's Word. The audience of nearly 600 ranges from 2 to 72 years in age and is spread out over a 50 yard area, so it's a fun challenge to create a message for Fridays.

I stole my illustration from Francis Chan, a superb preacher from California, but I included my personal favorite verse in the message—Philippians 3:10-11.

I started off the speech by having two dumbbells on a table and brought a sixth grader up. I told him that if he could lift the heavier one, I'd give him a chocolate brownie. I also asked the audience to decide mentally whether they thought he could or could not lift the heavier weight. Then, before I had him lift it, I got a third weight from my backpack that was twice as heavy as the heaviest one on the table. I told him that I just wanted to see if he could do that one before he lifted the other one for the prize. He almost couldn't do it (and honestly, if he hadn't been able to, it would have ruined my message), but

WINTER SPRING SUMMER FALL

switching to his right arm gave him just enough gusto to hoist it once.

The point of the illustration is that believing in God—the God of the Bible, the God who sent Jesus Christ, and the God who brought him back to life from death—is the heaviest, most serious, consequential decision we will make. If we believe in Him, then we believe in His power, His sovereignty, His holiness. Every other challenge or difficulty in life seems minute when compared with God's power as seen in the resurrection.

I used my own nervousness as an example. I wanted to be nervous about speaking in front of hundreds of people today. I wanted to worry and stress and be afraid. But if God truly has power over even death, if God has given me His spirit (that same Spirit that raised Jesus from the dead), then my stress is the equivalent of our wondering whether the sixth grader could lift the 15 lb. weight on the table. Since he had lifted the 30 lb. weight from my backpack, there is no question he could do half of that. If I believe that God raised Jesus from the dead, then I cannot question whether I'd be able to deliver a sufficient message (with adequate preparation and prayer beforehand, of course) because that power—the resurrection power—lives in me.

As always, we teach best that which we need to learn ourselves.

Later that afternoon, while walking home from class, a flood of worries and stress hit me, forcing me to ask the Lord for strength once again. Let me tell you what I was thinking, taken from "The Weight of the (Third) World," episode 10 of my podcast.[1]

My mom has been with us for the past three weeks, and I can't begin to tell you the help she's been. Without much time off of work for me, the adjustment to Asher in our world has

---

[1] My podcast *All That You Can't Leave Behind,* which shares its title with my first book, is available at *allthatyoucant.blogspot.com* and on iTunes.

proven to be uber-grueling (more on his birth in the "Stories for Living" section later in this chapter). Having Mom's help for three of the last six weeks of this term has been miraculous. Her exotic African trip has included laundry, cooking, cleaning, and childcare, all in the lush wilds of our apartment. Yes, she is getting to spend time with her two grandsons and Heather and me, but her use of vacation time (indentured servitude to her son's family) is probably considered rather sadistic by most.

To treat this sacrificial woman, Heather took her into Nairobi today with Asher and Micah for some sights and some food and some shopping. And here comes the part where I talk about my stress…

Walking home I began to think about my family in Nairobi. *Is the truck working okay? Have they been pulled over by the police* (there are at least 3 check points between here and the city)? *Are they staying clear of dangerous drivers? How are the boys feeling and handling the travel? Are they staying clear of thieves?*

Perhaps these worries seem natural to you. Perhaps you share them in California or Pennsylvania or wherever you are. Perhaps you think I'm irrational and overly negative.

But this singular example truly shows how different life is here. Problems may not happen daily for folks in Kenya, but there is a much higher likelihood of car accidents, run-ins with the police, and theft here than where you are.

Not a week goes by where I don't hear of a story of a car accident among missionaries here. Two missionary doctors in vehicles killed drunken pedestrians in two separate incidents in the past three months. And I know of two folks who have broken down cars right now. But it's not just a higher propensity for road problems which causes stress; it's the uncertainty that surrounds every incident—dangerous areas, encounters with the police, repair costs, fines, etc. A very normal "problem" in the States becomes a very difficult predicament in the Third World context.

43

All right, so I thoroughly explained one worry. Now, five or six steps closer to home, the next worry comes to light.

We're taking the night off because my mom's returning to the U.S. tomorrow night, and we're not chaperoning or hosting any student activities. On the one hand, we wish we could be spending the time with boarding students on campus, and there is that regret. They leave next Friday for a month, and we'll miss them. On the other hand, we know that the other staff here will have to work harder tonight (after experiencing the same intense week that we did) because of our absence. So there are two issues tugging at my heart, even though I know that we need to soak in every last minute with our far-off traveler.

Another few steps up the path to my house...

There's correspondence with family and supporters at home to get done by tomorrow so my mom can mail it for us from the U.S. where it's cheaper postage than from here.

And then there are the 75 seven-page research papers to be graded by next week.

And then there's dinner to be planned. With no Friday night pizza delivery or microwavable meals, the evening meal needs to be thought of and cooked from scratch just like every other meal. You have to start planning in the early afternoon if you want to eat before 8 o'clock at night.

Ok, why am I sharing this long excerpt? Looking for pity? Digging for admiration?

Hardly. One of the reasons I write is to share what life and faith is like for missionaries today. When something strikes me as unique, I talk about it so that you'll be able to get an inside perspective of missionary life.

My lesson for this chapter is that I live every day with a higher-than-normal stress level simply because of this line of work and being a stranger in Kenya. Sometimes I lose sight of that, and it builds up and it breaks down my heart and it gets inside the fabric of my days.

How do you handle stress? Do you constantly live with a high level of stress? Does stress come into your life in waves, with incredibly crushing peaks followed by long, luxurious valleys? Being ready for the missionary life means being ready for a never-ending crush of stress on your soul. I actually think it's impossible to handle the stresses of cross-cultural missions when we rely solely on our own capabilities and power.

And I don't want to lose sight of that because—here's the connection to my chapel message—I have the power through Christ to overcome my stresses. I have the strength to trust God with my stresses and worries because He has raised Jesus from the dead and gives me that power. I may have a higher stress level and more worries than I did before I came overseas, more than my 30-year-old male American counterparts have, but the resurrection power of God is enough to level my paths and to soothe my nerves. It's more than enough.

Stress can take a rest.

Stories of Living

The stories for this chapter focus on two of our most stressful experiences from our first term of service in Africa. "The Sting of Police" tells how the governments (namely police departments) of Third World countries challenge even law-abiding citizens with their use of bureaucratic power and create unavoidable stress. "One child, two parents, Third World" shares the experience of childbirth in Africa. After delivering our first son in the United States, my wife had no idea what to expect with #2—as if having a baby isn't stressful enough.

The sting of police

I've mentioned before how perilous the roads in Kenya are. Poor road conditions, untrained drivers, endless obstacles, and broken down vehicles are a few of the main culprits in this comedy of errors. But I think the biggest problem, I think, is the police.

You see, the police don't have vehicles. Vehicles are expensive in Kenya, and the government doesn't have a lot of money (or, should I say, doesn't have a lot of money that isn't dedicated to corruption) to spend on vehicles for their police. So, to maintain a presence out on the highways, they'll have roadblocks made of metal spikes. When you slow down they might pull you over, ask you questions, and cite you. In the cities, they'll use the normal traffic patterns to accost a slowed-down vehicle and do their thing.

They could cite you for pretty much anything they want. Sometimes they'll pull people over and accuse them of going over the speed limit. (Never mind the fact that they are not in a vehicle nor do they usually have radar guns.) Sometimes there will be another random infraction (like not having a light on your license plate frame, which isn't a real law), but whatever the reason, everyone in Kenya—natives included—knows they usually just want "chai money."[2]

Chai money is a euphemism for a small bribe. They usually don't demand much from the natives—maybe a dollar or two—because they know there's not a lot of money to be had. But when there is a mzungu (white) to pull over, they might be able to buy a whole lot of chai. Missionaries (at least ones I know) don't pay the chai money, which is not only the biblical response to corruption but also the best way to stop it from plaguing a country. If we get pulled over, we'll ask them to either write us a ticket to be paid in Nairobi (a *huge* hassle) or

---

[2] Chai is the most popular beverage in Kenya, comparable to coffee in the U.S. Chai breaks happen twice a day in the same manner of coffee breaks but practiced with more fervor. And by fervor, I mean that a pregnant woman shouldn't plan on delivering at precisely 10 a.m. or 3 a.m. if she wants assistance.

if they will let us pay on site, then we demand an official government receipt and their police badge numbers.

Like the police in the U.S., Kenyan police are most visible around the holidays or at certain times of the month. You know, the times when they need the extra money. Since they don't have cars, you'll rarely find them out and about on rainy days, and since Africa is so dangerous at night, you often won't find them on patrol after 6 p.m. either. Makes sense, right?

The byways, though, are the most common place to find the police. There is very little presence elsewhere. We've known of various robberies, beatings, and even murders in our surrounding community this year that have gone without justice. The only real action we've heard of from the police is when some citizens burned down a police officer's home because he shot a "lawbreaker." The locals wanted justice in the only way they could get it—the illegal way. However, the police weren't going to let this crime go without prosecution. Somehow, they were able to arrest 20 men in connection with this. Some are still in prison without trial after a year, but most were released within six (yes, 6!) months. Sometimes the police *can* track down criminals—if it suits their interest.

So, to summarize: there are large stretches of Kenyan roads without *any* law enforcement, and there are large periods of times when there is no law enforcement. They can't catch any lawbreakers because they don't have cars, and they are more interested in making some extra cash for themselves than keeping their country and its roads safe. And if you don't find a police officer near a road, you probably won't find one at all.

Don't get me wrong: the police could be worse. But they could be better too (I say with a wink).

Now, that I've introduced you to the Kenyan police, I'll tell you about my wife's little trip to the police station.

When you think of hardened criminals, you think of people like Charles Manson and John Gotti and Martha Stewart. Right? Okay, okay, maybe *you* don't think of Martha, but I do.

Anyway, back to my point. There is an image that comes to mind when you think of society's lawless. In Kenya, that image may be different than you'd expect.

Here it could be my wife. Heather.

Where I left off in my first book, Heather was newly pregnant. So, you can see, by this point in time, she's an even a *bigger* threat. (Don't tell her I joked about that.)

My wife and our co-worker Joan drove to Nairobi last week to pick up fabric for this weekend's band and choir concert tour from Rift Valley Academy. To do this, they had to go to a part of the city that neither of them knew very well. Making matters worse, Nairobi was hosting a huge environmental conference for Africa so the place was packed with drivers and pedestrians. And it was raining. After sitting in traffic for hours and getting little done, they suddenly found themselves in the wrong lane and headed into another traffic jam. Heather watched cars in front of her pull u-turns, and there were no signs anywhere. So, she u-turned aggressively, which is really the only way to drive in the city. And as she headed in the right direction, she saw the wrong man standing in front of her car. The policeman.

Heather pulled over. Well, not really. He stood in front of her in the road and made her stop right where she was. She blocked most of the traffic, which the police don't really care about, while he knocked on her back window. Yes, her back window. He wanted her to open up and let him in the car. After some debate (yes, you can debate with the authorities), they let the policeman and his female partner into the car. Next, he wanted them to pull another u-turn (yes, the same "illegal" procedure which they were being cited for) and go to the police station. While they debated some more, a half-dozen more cars pulled u-turns right in front of them. In the end, they hazardously followed his lawless advice and headed to the police station.

My wife. Pregnant. Heading to the downtown police station. In a Third World country.

Public enemy numero uno.

Their penalty was going to be 6000 shillings (90 dollars) which needed to be paid before they could be released that day and a court date scheduled for the next. Heather tried to look as big and pregnant as possible, and she waddled from our car to the police station praying for mercy. Joan talked and talked to the guy in the car and while they were walking. The ladies didn't have any money to pay the fine. The policeman said they should call a friend in Nairobi. Well, we live in Kijabe and don't have any friends in Nairobi yet. Then, he said he'd keep our vehicle as collateral, and we could find a way back to Kijabe to get the money. He put out his hands for the keys. Yeah right.

So, there they were, still outside the police station, and the cop turns to them and says, "OK, 5000 shillings and court date." Sound arbitrary to you? You got it. It was. The ladies sensed him backing off and continued to argue and plead. Finally the man turned to his female partner and talked. He turned back with good news.

He said to Heather, "My wife is pregnant and since you are pregnant too, I will let you go."

They thanked the officers profusely and went back to their frustrating day of errands, immensely relieved at not being fined and not having to lose another whole day dealing with legal matters.

In the end, Heather concluded that perhaps it truly was an act of compassion by the policeman. More likely however, the two cops needed a ride downtown (remember, they don't have cars) and didn't want to walk in the rain. They saw a comfortable vehicle and two white women and thought, "Easy prey." Probably hoping for a nice contribution towards their chai money, they blustered with a stiff fine and an inconvenient court date. When the women wouldn't go inside the police station and kept arguing, they got tired of standing out in the rain and decided they were satisfied that they got a ride out of the encounter. Heather went free, her first tussle with Kenyan police behind her, and the streets of Africa remain very dangerous.

My timid, gentle, and pregnant wife is still at large. Be afraid.

P.S. I don't want to cast the police in a totally negative light. Let me just add that I've had two positive experiences with police officers. One time I was speeding on this brand new road, probably the nicest road I've driven on since the I-8 freeway in San Diego, but the authorities had suspiciously set the speed limit at 50 kph (about 30 mph) on this asphalt heaven. I tried to go slow, but 80 kph (sing the *Dukes of* Hazzard theme with me now) is a little bit more than the law would allow. My father-in-law was in the car at the time, visiting us from California, and he laughs still today when he remembers the classic line that helped get me out of trouble—"Sir, it would make me very sad if you gave me a ticket." I guess the officer didn't want to make me sad.

The other encounter was over a more serious matter— my driver's license had apparently expired. Since theft is so common and procuring legal documents from the government such an arduous task, we carry only copies of the originals with us at all times. The copy I had in my wallet was two months past due, and I thought I was going to the slammer for this one. Again, I begged for mercy, and again (this time much more miraculously in my opinion), I received it. (When I got home and checked the original, everything was fine. It was updated, but my copy wasn't.)

I don't point out these positive experiences to brag about getting out of tickets. Kenyan police do a lot of good, and they have hard jobs. But both of these times, they granted a little bit of mercy and didn't dishonor themselves by asking for a bribe—honorable traits on both accounts.

One child, two parents, Third World

Often missionaries like us are dealt with in one of two ways. We're either vilified as self-righteous prigs who corrupt simple and pure people with our hellfire and brimstone religion and our overbearing Western culture. Or, we are placed high on a pedestal as saints just skimming the earth's crust, sacrificing pleasure and earthly desires for a higher calling to serve God. The one stereotype is way too mean-spirited, and the other a downright lie. Most missionaries I know are no better and no worse than most American Christians I know when it comes to personal ethics and spiritual maturity. The simple difference is that we've gone—we've made ourselves available for the hurting of the world. We shouldn't be elevated above anyone or cordoned off from the rest of our American brothers and sisters. But even the worst missionaries—past and present—aren't destroying anything that would justify the label of World Enemy #1.

While some of what we missionaries do involves heavy spiritual labor and intense service, a lot of what we do is mundane. Like cooking food. And doing laundry. And writing letters. And having babies. Stuff everybody does. Yes, these banal tasks may be universal and secular, but they are also individual and holy. Each life, filled with the ordinary and common, is made sacred by the intimate presence of a loving God.

So that's where my story fits in—a young American man trying to live in a strange land and to find God in the everyday living that dominates my "spiritual" vocation. And the "living" which was going on this day was the birth of our second child, a son we would name Asher Daniel. Although we planned on driving into the city for delivery at daybreak, the little guy didn't want to wait.

Once our friend Lauri arrived to spend the night with our almost-three-year-old Micah, Heather crawled into a nest of pillows and blankets in our backseat. We were the only car to be seen at that time of night in Kijabe (10 p.m.), and it wasn't until we arrived at the main road (5 miles up the hill) that we saw another. (Thieves are known to set up roadblocks on the road in

Kijabe, which is one reason there isn't much night travel in our area.)

There are few painted lines on the main road, and it's only two lanes (one in each direction). The speed limit is 100 kmh (about 60 mph), and although our emergency would have warranted going faster, I actually couldn't drive much faster than that at night and still feel safe. High beam etiquette isn't friendly in Kenya so crossing paths with oncoming vehicles is a hazard in itself. You can try to keep your eye on the left edge of the road, but then you have to worry about another motorist taking more than his share of the road and side swiping you.

There wasn't much conversation on that car ride. Heather was focusing on breathing, and she was in the zone. I'd ask her how she was doing or how far apart the contractions were, and she'd quickly say, "Okay. Need to breathe" or "Four minutes. Can't talk." But after about 45 minutes, she started to speak up.

"How long until we get there?"

Uh oh. Would we make it?

Two weeks ago our friendly Indian doctor, Dr Patel, looked at me with a smile and asked, "Ryan, have you been practicing how to deliver this baby?" I laughed. His smile stayed the same. *He was serious?* I didn't know how to respond so I told him that the only thing I was practicing was driving real fast to make it to the hospital in time.

Like a good 21st century man, I googled "How to deliver a baby" when I got home that day, printed out the results, and kept them in my wallet at all times. I also made up a bag with sterile sheets, a bulb syringe, and hand sanitizer. I labeled it "Dr. Ryan" so I'd be ready. Lucky for Heather, we made it to the real doctor in time, but not by much.

The bumps and swerves of our drive accelerated her contractions up from about 5 minutes apart when we left to almost 2 minutes. Her water still hadn't broken, but by the time we pulled up to the emergency room, we were certain Asher would be arriving at any moment. They took Heather off in a wheel chair and told me I had to go park elsewhere. Three minutes later, the same doctor and nurse who had just escorted my wife now had no clue who I was. After some discussions in Swahili, they realized which pregnant woman I belonged to and that they had taken Heather to the wrong wing of the hospital. They said they'd call upstairs and take her to the right wing and then pointed me in that direction.

When I sprinted up the stairs to the maternity floor, the nurses looked at me like I was nuts. They hadn't heard anything about a pregnant woman on the way. Now I was getting nervous. Was Heather giving birth to our son in some elevator or long hallway in this labyrinth of a hospital? Where was she?

Well, she did arrive a few minutes later, looking like she'd just gotten off the teacups at Disneyland. The good news was that the contractions had slowed down some. Asher gave us some time to breathe.

That would be the last time Asher would slow down, however. In his short existence, he gained and kept a reputation for being early. The three ways he was early? He came two weeks early, one day early, and fifteen minutes early (I'll explain shortly). My step-dad likes to joke that he was born in the morning so he could go to work on time. Perhaps Asher has inherited his work ethic.

He was two weeks early because his due date wasn't until February 25. Our India-born doctor weighs about 105 pounds with his three-piece suit on so I think he's culturally more comfortable with small women and small babies. Heather is a fairly tall American woman who birthed an 8 lb. 8 oz. baby already and so he'd been quite apprehensive about how big this one would be. I think he was expecting Arnold Schwarzenegger to emerge from Heather's womb. He shuddered when our 32-week ultrasound revealed at least a seven pounder already, so when Heather started dilating early (around 34 weeks) he was very relieved. We knew Asher wouldn't make it until the due date.

We planned on driving into Nairobi on Monday morning to induce labor, but as I said before, as soon as the sun went down on Sunday night, Asher started partying. Two weeks early wasn't early enough for him; he moved things up a day.

His last attempt at speeding up our timetable was when he arrived fifteen minutes before the doctor was ready. During an examination at around 3:30 a.m. on Monday morning, the doctor broke Heather's amniotic sac so the labor would intensify. She was starting to wear out, having not slept well in days and having not literally slept in 22 hours, and he wanted to help her along. But as he and his nurses prepared for the delivery, a storm was a-brewing in bed—the "transition" phase had begun.

Before I can talk about the near-*Poltergeist*-reenactment, I should explain how we got to a medication-free birth in Kenya's capital and not some other method of delivery.

Quite a few of our fellow missionaries in Kijabe have given birth in Kenya, and their experiences ranged from splendid to tragic. We took a lot of advice on how and where to deliver here...or should I say Heather got a lot of advice? I let Heather decide what she wanted to do with this pregnancy. Giving birth is traumatic and scary as it is, but having to do it in a foreign, Third World country is a-whole-'nother ball game. I was grateful she was giving me a second spawn; how she wanted to do it was her call.

Since some women had bad experiences with anesthesiology here and others had encouraged her to try it un-medicated, Heather decided to try the natural route. Although she could have delivered naturally at our local Kijabe hospital, even our doctor friends here recommended that we deliver in Nairobi. They are capable of delivering in Kijabe and successfully do so very often, but a few years ago a missionary woman had complications in her delivery and the baby died unnecessarily. Kijabe simply lacked the neo-natal care that Nairobi could provide. Chances are everything would have been fine close to home, but it wasn't a chance Heather felt all right about.

So, that's how we arrived at a natural childbirth in Nairobi, and that's how I came to find out about the "transition" stage.

Cue the theme music to Hitchcock's *Psycho*.

The transition stage is when the baby drops down the birth canal and presses its head right into the pelvis. It's the last step before the actual pushing begins, and it can last anywhere from 15 to 90 minutes. For most women, it's the most excruciating part of delivery, worse even than pushing the head through.

Up until this point, Heather had been the focused and peaceful monk through each contraction. She'd tell me to start timing and then she'd go into her trance, only to reemerge 50 seconds later with "It's over." They did grow in intensity and length as the night wore on, but Heather's demeanor was pretty much the same.

Let me make one more comment about pain and Heather. You could probably kick Heather in the shins right now, and she wouldn't make a peep. The only sign of anguish you'd see is a little tilt of the eyebrows. She's a silent sufferer. Her parents always tell the story of how when she was an infant her brother, who is two years older, would carry her around by the neck. They had no clue what was going on because Heather wouldn't make a peep. Her face certainly reflected mortal terror, but out of her mouth came not a sound.

However, a never-before-seen side of Heather came out during the transition phase. She was no longer St. Heather the Placid; she was Heather the Screaming Banshee of Perpetual Terror. Moaning, screaming, wailing, writhing, she squeezed my hands with unrelenting strength and wouldn't have heard my cries for "mercy" even if I had tried. This side of her was so bizarre and unusual for her that I almost laughed, which probably would have killed my bid for husband-of-the-year.

She even tried to bite me. At first I didn't pull away, assuming my tranquil wife could never do something so barbaric, but when she opened her mouth, I slowly slipped my arm away and let her rest her ravenous teeth on the plastic railing of the bed for a second.

After the transition phase, Asher came quickly, almost before the doctor was ready. The pediatrician who was called to attend didn't even make it. Fifteen minutes after his birth, the woman doctor rolled in to check out the early bird.

Those 45 minutes, from when her water broke to the transition phase to the delivery, were some of the most surreal of my life. As we look back now, even she laughs at her unexpected behavior. But my amusement is definitely punctuated by amazement, amazement at the pain of childbirth and the strength of my wife to go through the entire thing naturally.

I think the strangest thing about our second child's arrival was how different it was from our first. As we spent two days in the hospital hanging out with Asher and retreating from the intensity of our teaching ministry at the boarding school, the contrasts kept coming to us one after another.

First off, the drive. We lived a 15-minute freeway ride away from the hospital where Micah was born. Smooth roads, cruising 65 mph the whole way, and any time of the day was fine for driving. Here, we live an hour away from the hospital. The two-lane road was a bumpy nightmare for my 38 week pregnant wife, and we took a risk by driving at night in Africa. The long drive was one of the reasons we wanted to induce labor a week early, but in the end, our planned attempt at picking the birth date didn't work for Asher as it did for Micah.

Secondly, Micah was born at a great hospital in one of the best cities in the US while Asher was born in a great hospital in one of the best cities in Africa. Now I'm not about to gripe about what kind of care we got here; the facilities and professionalism in Nairobi really were great. Was Nairobi equal to San Diego? No. The best in Africa isn't equal to the best in America. I'll leave it at that.

Thirdly, the family difference. Micah's birth was two clowns short of a circus (and if my sister and dad had been there, the circus would have been complete). We had over a dozen folks in the waiting room ready to descend upon our new arrival as soon as he hatched. Cousins, friends, parents, mentors, uncles and aunts...even the medical staff was a bit overwhelmed by the welcome committee Micah had for his birth. Asher's birth was the other extreme. One missionary friend in Nairobi came to visit us the day after his birth. Unfortunately there was no family there, and the Barnum and Bailey atmosphere never erupted.

Fourthly, I took two weeks off when Micah was born. I took three days off for Asher. We don't have substitute teachers at Rift Valley Academy; everyone is stretched thin as it is so taking just one day off is a burden. At Grossmont High School, I had one great lady cover my classes for two weeks, worry-free. Here, there were at least five different people covering for all my different responsibilities, probably more.

Even though we'd been through a birth before, we certainly learned a few more things with Asher's coming. The first lesson—birth goo is your friend.

They didn't really wash Asher off for us after his birth, so as we held him in our arms for the first time, we watched the white stuff and the red stuff and the brown stuff dry right on to his skin. Not that we really cared that we had a dirty baby; we had a healthy baby and that was enough for us. But it was still kind of weird.

Lesson #2: Babies turn out best when cooked at 200 degrees. The nurses in Nairobi thought it really important to whisk the baby away from the parents immediately after birth and get them under heat lamps. Heather wasn't too cognizant at that point, still reeling from the whirlwind of "transition" labor, but I was a bit miffed. I went into the nursery with him for a while, until I couldn't stand the heat any longer. Not only was

Asher's crusty little body swaddled, they had him directly under these two glowing-red, toaster oven-like heat lamps. Maybe 200 degrees is an overstatement, but I still think Asher's going to have a nice tan for the rest of his life because of those things.

Another thing we learned during our hospital stay—All white people look the same. As our two new nurses started their shift, they came into introduce themselves and laughingly told us that all three of us—Heather, Asher, and myself— looked the same. White people all look the same to Kenyans; we'd heard it before, and they just wanted to let us know that again. To further teach this lesson, every time I walked up the stairs to the maternity floor, the security guards stopped me and asked which room I was visiting. Even as I packed up the car on our last day, the guards couldn't tell one white man from another. "Sir, which room are you going to?"

The last lesson we learned was on the last day of our stay. Some friends of ours at Rift Valley Academy brought our almost 3-year-old to meet his baby brother for the first time. As Micah took my hand and walked into the hospital room, I realized how fast the last three years have gone. This coordinated, intelligent, articulate, golden-brown-haired boy was in Asher's state not too long ago—a flailing, crying, bony, sleepy little bundle of breath. The days do fly by, and we don't want to take even one day for granted.

SPRING

Lessons for Lasting
Laughter

Genesis 21:5-6
"Abraham was a hundred years old when his son Isaac was born to him. Sarah said, 'God has brought me laughter, and everyone who hears about this will laugh with me.'"

In my book *All That You Can't Leave Behind*, I wrote about the triumphs and traumas of becoming a cross-cultural missionary. One story detailed the purchase of a vehicle in Kenya and how relationships are foundational for conducting business. It's important to be polite and friendly in all that you do, even if your business partner is lying, cheating, or stealing from you. That's etiquette here.

Learning a culture is truly a never-ending process. The way you're hardwired as a child and then as a young adult establishes instincts within you stronger than a rip tide. You want to zig when the new culture says zag; when you're ready to zag, then they start zigging. But as a missionary, you have to study the way your host countryman is hardwired, and you need to tackle your own behavioral circuitry as well to figure out why you want to backhand someone when they snicker at you for simply saying thank you. Aren't manners a good thing, you wonder? If you want to love people in God's name, you have to love them as they understand life and love.

As I try to figure out this balance, I find myself teetering between seething rage and out-loud laughter. There really is little room in between. A new culture will drive you certifiably insane if you don't find a way to laugh at yourself and your predicament.

Currently, I have three "business" dealings that are teaching me that I much prefer American etiquette to Kenyan etiquette. I'll try to explain without foaming at the mouth and driving my fist through my laptop. Procuring a birth certificate, fixing a broken computer, and installing extra seats for our vehicle are the three current situations that are driving me batty.

I'll start with the birth certificate. Asher was born a little over three months ago now, and the hospital submits the paperwork to the government for us to obtain a birth certificate. Without a birth certificate we can't get a passport, and without a passport, we can't leave the country with our son. To help us with the frustrations of dealing with the government (sporadic business hours, wasted trips to Nairobi, and wasted time standing in lines), we hired a Kenyan to be our liaison. About once a week he stops in and checks on the paperwork's progress for us. He's also filed a few papers for us to keep the process moving, but still no birth certificate. I call him (never the other way around[1]) about once a week, and he tells me the bad news every time. "Not done yet." Finally, yesterday, they told him that June 6th would be the date it would be done. Getting an official date is good, but I wouldn't place even a 5-shilling bet that the saga will conclude then.

Okay, on to Frustration #2—fixing our computer.

I'm typing now on our laptop, but our real workhorse computer (for video editing, pictures, emails, music, newsletters) started having problems a few months ago. Then, the Internet stopped working altogether. Minor problem, or so I thought. In the process of trying to restore it, our tech geek

---

[1] The reason no one returns your call is that everyone has cell phones, on which it is free to receive a call—even from overseas—but it's not free to place a call. In the U.S., it's downright rude to not return call after call, but here, I'm seen as the rich white person and they want to save their money. The etiquette for phone calls is different.

friend Mike made a mistake. The new problem was too big for him to fix, so we took it to Nairobi for more help. It's been there for over two weeks now, but not because the problem is so insurmountable. Rather than work on our computer until it is done, they are working on it *pole pole* (Swahili for "slowly, slowly"). Every day when I call to see how it's coming, the worker says, "Call back in an hour," which means, "I haven't worked on it today so let me see what new problem I can encounter in the next hour so I can tell you that it's not done." Every day. Two weeks. No computer. I foot the bill for every call.

But the last situation takes the cake. Oh yeah, this one is legendary.

About three months ago, we began searching for a craftsman who could make extra seats for our vehicle. Everybody in America has SUV's but mainly for different reasons than we do in Africa. I cruised around San Diego for seven years in a 1991 Jeep Cherokee, mostly by myself. I probably used the 4WD twice in those seven years and needed the high clearance an SUV provides less than a dozen times. Here, not only do we need the clearance and 4WD, but rarely do we go anywhere without a full car. Rides to the city are hard to find because few people own vehicles. Few people own vehicles because vehicles costs are lucrative here and faith-based missionaries aren't *Forbes* magazine cover boys and girls. Extra seats in our Toyota LandCruiser would mean we could help more missionaries and nationals with transportation.

It took us weeks to even locate someone to add seats to our SUV. Hardly anyone does these kinds of modifications, but eventually we found someone in Nairobi who said they'd take him three days to make. He didn't even need us to come in for measurements; he had our exact vehicle himself. Well, four days passed, and we called him. He said maybe tomorrow. We called the next day. And the next. We were still encouraged though. The price was right and waiting a week was what we expected at the beginning anyway.

Finally, he said they were almost done. He was going to pick them up the next day from his manufacturer, and we could have them installed the next afternoon. The next day we drove to Nairobi and hung out, passing the time until he called and we could meet him. The afternoon had almost passed and we called him. The seats were completed, but not up to the quality he wanted. We wouldn't be getting the seats today.

For the next two weeks, we'd call him and either get his voice mail or be told, "Call me tomorrow." Finally, after about a month of waiting for this guy, I had enough. Even though there was no Plan B, I told him that we were taking our business elsewhere, hoping that my bluff would provoke service. No such luck. He told me I should go elsewhere.

The search for a craftsman resumed. After another two weeks, I found someone else. The price was about the same, and again I was told confidently that they'd be done in a few days. That was two weeks ago. The last word I heard was, "They'll be done on Monday or Tuesday."

No, I'm not holding my breath.

Our friends Matt and Robyn are here right now working as dorm parents, and Matt does a lot of odd jobs in the U.S. He said to me, "These people wouldn't stay in business one week in the States," and he's totally right. The incompetence and inefficiency of business here in Kenya is only eclipsed in size by the apathy. And how can they be apathetic?

One, lack of competition. There is a low supply of skilled workers to do what we need done here. The worst workers in the U.S. don't get business. The worst workers here may be the *only* workers. And when shoddy work is done, it's culturally awkward to tell anyone they've done wrong. You hurt someone's reputation by saying they've done wrong. Getting over that cultural hurdle is no easy task.

Two, different ideas about customer service. The customer is *not* always right here. The person providing service is higher on the food chain than the customer; they are employed and in a country with an unemployment rate at over

60%, that makes them the lucky ones. The consumer should stand in awe at the greatness of the service provider.

The third conclusion I've come to about Kenyan business is their apathy is directly related to a lack of ambition. The American Dream is to work harder and get richer. This rule works for everyone, whether on minimum wage or a mega-billionaire, and it drives American advertising. It seems like the Kenyan dream is to get enough. Why should they work harder than they are currently? Why should they care about having a great business reputation if they are getting enough business right now? If their pockets are currently full, why worry about business tomorrow?

My three observations have helped my blood pressure stay below the volcanic level as, I have to admit, I struggle to simply laugh off these cultural differences as part of the joys of missionary life. But that's really what it comes down to.

From outside a culture, you can see how insane the culture is. From inside, you get carried along for the ride. Like a passenger standing on a bus, you think you're standing still, perfectly balanced, without a care, until the driver taps his breaks. Suddenly, you're shocked into reality—I'm traveling 50 miles an hour while standing still! After you pick yourself up off the ground, you have two options—either laugh at the ridiculous notion of your own stability or stomp your feet at the injustice of the laws of inertia and gravity.

In missions, we're faced with the same choice. Spend our days stomping feet over the injustice and illogical nature of foreign cultures or laughing at the ridiculous cultural differences we're faced with.

If you're looking for profound depth from this lesson, you won't find it. Actually, this whole chapter might be a washout for you. But remember, this chapter is about laughter, a very important aspect of missionary life.

The key passage for this chapter comes from a story about a couple that couldn't get pregnant for at least 60 years and then—after hundreds of misses—finally got it right. The news comes to them in Genesis 18:1-15 and ends in laughter. At first, she laughs in disbelief, but by the time the child is born and God's message to them comes true, her laughter is a laugh of acceptance and praise. Breastfeeding and waking up in the middle of the night and lugging around a chubby baby probably would have been easier forty years earlier or so, but Sarah accepts the wackiness of God.

If we can't laugh at ourselves and our crazy lives, we'll probably lose our minds as missionaries. We don't know the language. We dress differently. We act differently. We have a different worldview. We believe and serve a God and religious system that is foreign to everyone around us. Missions is a crazy idea.

But it's God's idea. So, you and I do it and laugh and accept, like Sarah, that "everyone who hears about this will laugh with me." And it's my firm conviction that having a sense of humor about life doesn't lessen the importance of reaching out to a lost world. It doesn't diminish God's glory in the slightest; what it does do is allow us to find joy in all of God's plans, even the improbable and seemingly impossible.

So I'll take my three little observations about Kenyan culture, try to keep a good sense of humor, and pick up my cell phone one more time. I'll call these "service providers" and beg them to provide me with service someday. And maybe tomorrow they'll give me a new excuse.

Or maybe they'll just tell me, "Call back tomorrow." You gotta laugh.

Stories of Living

If you're looking for a chortle, a snort, or a guffaw, you've come to the right place. First, it's a long road from pig to Easter ham. I'll take you down more of that road than you'd probably like in "The life and times of an Easter ham." Then, traditions rarely make sense to outsiders, and in "Traditions" I'll talk about some of the oddest ones at our boarding school. Finally,

I'll share the funniest things I've heard uttered this season with "Laughter is the best medicine."

The life and times of an Easter ham

Edward, a Kenyan man who raises pigs as a side job, told us on Thursday that he was slaughtering two the next day. His wife begins another semester of school to become a teacher and tuition is due Monday, which means it was time for him to cash out on two of his investments—Porky and Babe. I wanted to help him out, so I bought a fourth of a pig.

Problem. I don't know how to butcher a pig.

Solution. I paid Edward a little extra money, and he came to my house and showed me the ropes after his other pig deliveries.

In the meantime, the quarter-pig resided on the counter in our laundry room, which I thought was ripe material for a good joke. My wife, unaware that I was purchasing pork that wasn't shrink-wrapped on a styrofoam tray, came into the kitchen innocently enough, until I told her to take a look in the back. It took a second for it to register that she was looking at dead animal's leg and hind end. When it did, I got a good laugh and a solid slap on the arm.

Edward returned soon afterwards, and it was amazing. As he went through the process, he says, "This is the part to use for bacon, this for ham, this for tenderloin, this for pork cubes, etc." It was like walking through the aisle of a butcher shop, and all I was doing was looking at one side of a pig. As we went along, the side of this pig (which looked, not surprisingly, like the side of a pig) began to look like purchasable, cookable, eatable food. The cut that ends up on our plate really doesn't look like the animal it starts out on, I learned.

Here's my meditation—I'm glad that God still doesn't require a blood sacrifice for our sins. I'm glad I don't have to see dead animals every time I want some beef stew or hot dogs (if in fact hot dogs come from animals) because I don't like death too much. Just to think that this poor little piggie was slopping around gleefully yesterday, and now his four parts are scattered through kitchens throughout our campus. And I think Edward boiled his head for soup. Meat is gruesome stuff.

But when I consider how revolting the blood and death of an animal is to me, I think of the massacres that have happened throughout history—the machetes in Rwanda, the gas chambers of the Holocaust, the torturous executions of Communist Russia. All of those deaths, all of those sins.

And then I think of God and how He had just one Son who was not only made in His image but had God's very own DNA. "For in Christ all the fullness of the Deity lives in bodily form" (Colossians 2:9) and yet God, the awesome...the immortal...the omnipotent...had to allow His Son to bleed and writhe and die for our sins to be atoned...for many sons to come to glory.

For our salvation.

If God loved us so much that He'd allow the butchering of His only Son, then the filthiness of our sins must be worse than we think. Our sin is far more revolting and reviling than the death and slaughter of sheep and cows and pigs; our sin is so revolting that the death of God Himself must pay for it.

Despite the gruesome nature of the redemption story, the Easter story, Sunday morning is pure and white and clean. The power of God transcends the human drama of pain and blood and struggle and death. God overcomes the grave and raises us to life. To Him, we were worth the work.

Enjoy your ham this Easter. I know I will. It was worth the work.

Traditions

A 17-year-old boy breaks through a crowded hallway, screaming and flailing. He knows the rules of school, and normally he's a good kid, but he's being pursued, hunted, and tracked. He knocks over a girl half his size, and she falls to the ground, stunned. She seems to be all right. The other students look on with smiles once he's gotten past them, unconcerned by his behavior, although an outsider might think this was a traumatic matter of life and death. The predator that he's running from wields no weapon, only a scarf, a scarf that is intended to go around his neck.

The tradition I just described is called "scarfing." It happens every year before the junior class's last party of the school year. The week before the party, each girl wears a scarf to school, and her goal is to wrap her scarf around the neck of the guy who will be her "date" to the party. One might think it was rude for boys to be running from girls or overly aggressive for girls to be chasing down their men, but it's simply a game. The guys want to be the last one to be unscarfed, and the girls want to be without their scarves as early in the week as possible.

I don't know how far back this ritual goes, but it's a big enough deal that there are rules posted for all contestants. Here are a few of the most interesting of the "Ten Commandments of Scarfing":

> 3. Thou shall not scarf above or below the neck, only scarves residing between the chin and shoulders are valid.
> 5. Thou shall use violence as a last resort *only*
> 6. Thou shall not use mobs. Definition of mob: 20+ people.
> 9. If thou art scarfed, thou shall wear the scarf until class party.

While Rift Valley Academy is notorious for its many rules (to keep 500 kids in line without their parents around surely needs a strong system of order), these are the fun kind of rules. But playing this game by the rules means sometimes that other rules (real rules) are broken. Like the kid mentioned above who ran through the hall and bowled over a small girl, or the kid who didn't go to class because a mob-minus-one was waiting for him by the door. Yeah, he got a D-Hall (detention) for the infraction, but it was worth it to him to get one day further in the game.

Another tradition around here is "banquet asking." Banquet is essentially prom without the dancing and after-parties. Juniors and their parents plan and prepare for the event, and it truly is a once-in-a-lifetime event for our students. Seniors have no responsibilities for the event except to dress up and have a good time, relishing the fact that their junior year and all of the preparation that went into banquet is over.

Because of the excitement and hype around this event, guys are not allowed to ask girls until six weeks before the event. That way if anyone breaks up with someone or changes their mind or any other dramatic turn of events, the trauma only lasts a short while. But on that morning when banquet asking begins…look out. Boys call dorms at 6:00 a.m. to "reserve" the right to ask a girl, and boys that call at 6:01 are left out in the cold. And why would they simply want to reserve the right? Why wouldn't they ask right then and there? Well, banquet asking has become an event to rival marriage proposals.

Once the boy has reserved a girl (with the 6 a.m. call), then he can go through with his plan to her ask to banquet. Roses simply aren't enough. Perhaps the most elaborate "asking" of late was a missionary pilot who dropped a package out of the sky onto the school's field during an event. The boy took the girl out to retrieve it, and inside the box was a letter with the question, "Will you go to banquet with me?" Another extremely creative "asking" was a boy who gave a girl a box of cereal, printed in color with her picture and name on it. Inside the box was not only a delectable and rare American sugar cereal (Lucky Charms, I believe) but a note popping the big question to his date. She said yes.

Girls usually don't say no, so as not to offend the boy asking (who is, at the very least, a friend and usually is a close friend). This is why the 6 a.m. calls to "reserve the right" happen. And of course, there are the occasional hard feelings when a guy has talked about and planned and prepared to ask a certain girl, and another beau swoops in minutes before to steal the damsel. But all is fair in love and war, right?

(Perhaps the women's lib movement is finally coming to our school though, as this year there were a rash of girls who actually said no to the first asker. Bra burning is surely just around the corner.)

RVA has a myriad of other traditions that don't deal with girls and guys and dating though. Like Titchie Weekend (elementary school festivities where parents frequently visit) and Senior Store (delicious food prepared as a fundraiser for seniors) and Interim (juniors' and seniors' week-long off-campus excursions). But the worst tradition of all, and I'll probably take some flack for writing this, is a song that is sung every year at graduation—Toto's "Africa."

Presumably, this song snuck into a graduation ceremony in the early eighties (with its lyrics modified to make it more spiritual and coherent), and it hasn't gone away. Who knows what this song is actually about? Yet parents and students get teary-eyed every year while this pop relic is sung by our choir. Is it catchy? Yes. Is it the grand finale I'd want to cap off my high school career? Hold on a second, while I control my laughter.

Traditions. Sometimes silly, sometimes touching. Always rooted in a missionary kid's heart.

Laughter is the best medicine

Reader's Digest has a weekly sidebar called "Laughter is the best medicine" which includes jokes sent in by their readers. It's a nice, relaxing break from all of the intense articles about being trapped on top of a mountain and dying from rare fungi. My Grandpa Workinger got me a subscription as a kid, and I read those serious articles occasionally, but I think "Laughter is the best medicine" was the only column I read religiously.

In the same vein, I don't want my readers to get too weighed down by the weight of the mission world. So, I reflected on the funniest things said during the past school year. Here they are in no particular order.

"He is now a man." Our son Asher was born in a Kenyan hospital in February, and we asked them to follow the American custom of circumcision after birth. In Kenya, however, they still follow the custom of circumcision as a rite of passage from boyhood to manhood—it usually happens at around 16. So, when the Kenyan doctor emerged from surgery with my son on the day after his birth, he brings the swaddled boy to me and pronounces, "He is now a man." I got the joke.

"I Married a Cannibal." Although Rift Valley Academy is an American school, we get missionary kids from all over the world—Brazil, South Korea, South Africa, Norway, and even Canada (just kidding, eh!). Some have known English all their lives, but many are still gaining fluency in tenth grade English. One Dutch student has spoken English for years, but this is her first year learning in an English-speaking school. During her book report in the fall, her accent was so thick that I was struggling to follow the plot. I couldn't even make out the title. At the end of the speech, I embarrassedly asked her if the title was *I Married a Cannibal.* She laughed and said, "No, it was *I Marched with Hannibal.*" Much different book. Much, much different book.

"Those pants look so soft." I had my coaching debut in fall of 2006, coaching the junior high girls' basketball team, and man, I poured my heart into it. I ran those girls and yelled and taught them every ounce of hoops wisdom I had to impart. One day, in the middle of an important lesson on the importance of setting solid screens to defeat a zone defense, I asked if there were any questions or comments that the girls had about the skill we were learning. Sarah raised her hand and pointed to my legs: "Those pants look so soft." I then realized that I was coaching girls and not boys. Rather than soaking in the knowledge that would help them defeat and destroy the opposing teams, they were admiring fabric textures.

And finally, to bring this season full circle, a little tale of cultural confusion and comedy. My language helper Boniface borrows DVDs from us occasionally. He asked me last week if he had returned the last two videos he borrowed. I asked him which two they were. I thought he said, "A lot of things." So, I asked him again, "What were the videos?" He said again (I thought), "A lot of things."

Now, I was confused. Why wouldn't he tell me their names? And I thought he said there were only *two* videos...now he's telling me there are a lot of them? He said, "No, there were just two." I was starting to get frustrated and I asked, "Why did you say there were a lot of them?" He said as clearly as he could, "They're a lot of things!"

Finally, I just stopped in the path (we were walking and talking) and said, "What are you talking about?" Then, we were able to figure it out.

Many cultures have trouble pronouncing the hard "R" of the English language. It often sounds like "L." And if they have trouble with our "L" it often comes out sounding like "R". (Remember that classic scene in *A Christmas Story* when they eat Christmas dinner in a Chinese restaurant to the sounds of "Fa-ra-ra-ra-ra ra-ra-ra ra" sung by Asian waiters?) The "D" and "T" sounds are also closely related phonetically. So, having said that, let's insert some "R" and "D" sounds into "a lot of things."

Figured it out yet? I'll give you a hint—hobbits, dwarves, and "my precious."

"A lot of things" was actually *The Lord of the Rings*. Maybe Kikuyu would be easier for me to learn if we both spoke English the same way.

Part Two

SUMMER

Lessons for Lasting
Humility

Hebrews 12:1
"Therefore, since we are surrounded by such a great cloud of witnesses, let us throw off everything that hinders and the sin that so easily entangles, and let us run with perseverance the race marked out for us."

My midterm break for this season didn't really feel like much of a weekend. It was more like an out-of-body experience.

As soon as school let out on Friday, my friend Matt and I drove three Kenyan friends (Earnest [sic], Daniel, and Samuel are their English names) to their home area about 5 hours away. Earnest, a seminary graduate taught by missionaries in Kenya, is the first friend I made when I moved to Africa. As luck would have it, his first job after seminary was as chaplain of the hospital near our school, and our friendship has continued. He'd been looking for a way to take his strange white buddy home with him, and it finally happened.

The journey would have been nearly impossible after dark so we stopped at a friend's house half way to Earnest's home. The next morning we awoke and finished our journey. We drove through streams and over boulders and through ruts and mud. We felt like stars in an SUV commercial as we zigzagged up the mountain. Fortunately, the weather was excellent, as rain or heat could have complicated our trip. Crystal clear skies provided one magnificent view after another.

Another reason we felt like stars was the attention we got as we journeyed. We've grown quite accustomed to stares everywhere we go in Kenya, but this particular area was so remote and mountainous that only a handful of whites are seen each year in the entire region.

The welcome was warm in Mbooni (just say "bony" and you'll be close enough), as Earnest's parents had not seen him in a few months. Also, the sight of visitors brought smiles to the family's faces. Kenyans have an extremely gracious sense of hospitality, and since we were so unusual (white American missionaries) the greeting was extra gracious. Relatives from all over the hillside walked to Earnest's house to meet us.

They offered us a buffet of traditional Kenyan foods (not differing much from what the people of Kijabe eat), and Matt and I were graciously given the gizzard—a traditional gift for the guest at a meal. We quietly passed it off to a thankful Earnest later in the meal when no one was looking. After sitting around and talking for a few hours, they then showed us the beautiful sights of their area, including a breathtaking 180 degree view of the valley extending hundreds of miles to the mountain ranges in the distance.

The next morning we awoke early for church, and Earnest boiled water for us to bathe with. Their brick outhouse has two rooms—on the right a long drop (a hole used as a toilet) and on the left a room with a small pipe in the corner for bathing. The outdoor bath went pretty well, but the soap was a bit stickier than we had imagined and didn't come off entirely even when we had emptied our bowl of warm water. I don't think daily showers would be an American habit if this were the necessary routine.

We thought we were making good time until Earnest got a phone call saying that the church service where we were to speak began a half hour earlier. I quickly drove over the rugged terrain, and we arrived at the high school where six hundred boys were worshiping and awaiting their guests.

Mbooni Boys' School was our first stop of the day. Earnest graduated from there, and they were glad to welcome back an alumnus and current pastor. Even though it was an honor to have Earnest return, Matt and I were the truly unusual guests so we were invited to speak at both Mbooni and at the Africa Inland Church (AIC) later in the day. If forced to choose between public speaking and death—most people's two greatest fears—Matt would rather be in the coffin, so I willingly picked up both of the preaching opportunities. I talked about how we devote ourselves—our time, money, and thoughts—to things that will actually destroy us, partially or totally. In the book of Joshua in the Bible, God killed people for this kind of disobedience of His commandments, so I don't think He's changed His attitude from handing out death penalties to gently smirking at our half-devoted obedience. Yet in our modern churches, the picture of God smiling and wagging his finger playfully at us is popularly perpetuated. If we're not killing sin in our lives, sin will be killing us.

The service went great, and our brief chai with the headmaster of the school afterwards was an honor. But the second service was really magical.

The AIC church where Earnest grew up was a piece of living history. The first Africa Inland Mission missionaries started on the coast (Mombasa) and headed inland, through wilderness and mountains. On this particular mountain in 1905, missionaries stopped and built a strategic church on top of a hill overlooking two small valleys and one vast one. One of the church elders pointed with pride towards a distant hill and told me the story of how the white man walked from that direction until he stopped at the very spot where we now stood. He was so animated in his telling that I expected someone to emerge again any second. His pride was overwhelming, both in their faith's short history and in the fact that he was talking to a current missionary.

Like I said, not a lot of whites make it all the way to their mountain anymore. Not only is it out-of-the-way, it's also hard to get to. I thought I was simply visiting another African church, just like I've done countless times before. I figured I'd be warmly greeted, like every other time, but that'd be it. At Mbooni, however, visiting with me was like connecting with the treasured past for them. I had no idea how transcendent this experience would be for me.[1]

Now I'm not a preacher or an evangelist, but it was all the same to them. I preached to them for 30 minutes on how belief can overcome fear, and to them, it was like 1905 all over again. I spoke through a translator so that the older members (like the 97 year old man who actually knew the original missionary family, the Lourdes family, which began the church one hundred years prior) could understand what I was saying, and then Matt and I enjoyed meeting with all of the members at a luncheon right there at the church.

If my time at the church in Mbooni reminded them of the past, it reminded me of the future. All over Africa on this very day, new churches are being planted by Africans and by missionaries. Africans are watching white men (and yellow men and brown men and other black men) come into their villages for the first time (maybe not by foot anymore, but by car or by plane) for the first time and wondering what they're up to. Memories, like the ones of the church I visited, will be passed down for generations of how the Gospel of grace came to each new people group.

And as a teacher of missionaries' kids, I get to be part of that process. Perhaps a hundred years from now, a naïve white man from America will walk into a remote tribe and be told the

---

[1] The ultimate goal of missions is to plant self-sustaining, indigenous churches among a people group. Once that goal is met, there will still be partnership between the new church and Christians outside the church, but there is not a need for an on-going missions presence. The church in Mbooni is one such success story. Missionaries didn't abandon these people; they built a healthy church that didn't need missionaries anymore.

story of one of my colleagues and how he began a church in 2007 that has stood and grown for one hundred years.

Whatever your role is in worldwide missions, knowing about those who have gone before us is a crucial discipline. You and I didn't invent this stuff. It's been going on for millennia now. We walk in the shadows of giants of the faith, and a proper understanding and respect for those who went before is due.

Their stories will energize us to work harder, give deeper, and love longer. Their lives will motivate us to take up our crosses and die daily, like the writer of Hebrews 12:1 says.

Knowing our place in the great "cloud of witnesses" also makes us small. Small in a good way. We may one day feel like we're really important because of the ministry we're doing. We may start to think somehow like we're doing something that no one else could do. We may think the kingdom of heaven really needs us around. But like the water droplets in a cloud, we are very insignificant on our own. When we place ourselves in proximity with all the other witnesses, then together we form a cloud that will one day cover the whole earth. It's good to be small when we're part of something big.

Past, present, and future collide. The Old Testament witnesses, the New Testament followers, and every believer on every continent today. Jonah preaching to the Ninevites, Paul speaking in Athens, Hudson Taylor penetrating China, and my miniscule self teaching in Africa. It's all the fabric of one big story. And Jesus Christ is the same hero through them all.

Stories of Living

Summer time is vacation time for Westerners. The first two stories focus on two trips that I took during our Kenyan summer (which is actually cool and rainy, not hot and dry). The third story isn't about a holiday, but it is about relief—the conclusion to my "Lesson for Lasting" about laughter from last spring.

Are you ready?

You'll have to excuse me for this bit of anachronistic storytelling, but this revelation came to me right before my trip to Mbooni.

As I prepared for three days and two nights away from home with Earnest—a weekend living *like* the Kenyans whom I live *among* every day—I did the typical American thing: I ran through a checklist in my head of things I'd need while I was gone. The only difference was that this checklist had to be complete. The place where we were headed was so remote that there would be no toothbrush or bar of soap at a corner 7-11.

And so I spent a good 30 minutes longer than I normally would packing, teasing out every conceivable scenario, envisioning what life would be like in the house of rural Kenyans. More and more things came to mind, things that could help me have a more comfortable and pleasurable weekend. And while they did, my bag got fuller and fuller. But that was no problem. If my bag overflowed, I had the back seat of my SUV to catch the spillage.

My brain scanned over its own "needs" list continuously until I began to back out of my driveway. At that point, I realized how obsessive I am, how obsessive I believe Americans are, when it comes to being un-needy.

The reason I wanted to be "prepared" for this weekend, was so that I wouldn't need anything. I wanted to be self-sufficient as I traveled hundreds of miles and didn't want to get in any situation where I'd need someone's help or gifts. Although the journey was to be difficult, I wanted to be able to succeed by myself, on my own strength, and with my own wisdom to be credited with the victory.

This is such a metaphor for my spiritual life. I don't want to be needy, even when it comes to my relationship with God. I want to be able to do it all on my own, even the hardest things, so that I can get the credit for the good I've done—credit both from God and from men.

I catch myself all the time praying silly, selfish words like, "Lord, please give me a good day," words that sound fine on the surface, but when you peel just one layer back, you find a desire for un-neediness. In reality I'm saying, "Lord, please let this day be easy so that I don't need You." Even the prayer itself is a way of packing up my metaphorical bags, as some part of me thinks that praying such a prayer will be a ticket to a comfortable, independent day.

Kenyans aren't afraid to be needy. Plainly and straightforwardly asking for what they need or want is natural to them. Of course, this is one of the cultural traits that most irks Westerners (and irks me!) about living among them. It takes such radical and desperate humility for us to ask for help—financially, emotionally, spiritually—that we shudder at the thought of being needy in everything as a way of life. Yet that's how my Kenyan brothers and sisters live. And it's not only for physical things—money, food, jobs—but it's for spiritual things as well. Those who are sincere Christians (and there are many) will beg for God's provision as naturally as you or I breathe. Neediness is life.

But for me, self-reliance is a way of life. Bag filled with snacks, jugs filled with water, spare tire inflated, extra toilet paper rolls, cash-stuffed wallet, changes of clothing, two pairs of shoes in case of rain, and the list goes on. While I'd usually think of that list and say, "Attaboy, Ryan. Way to be prepared," I now simply shake my head and say, "Ryan, Ryan, Ryan…you need so much more than that. If only you could see…"

Holy days

I'm sitting about 1 kilometer from the Indian Ocean right now. It was sunny and 90 thirty minutes ago; now it's rainy and 70. Gotta love tropical weather. We didn't think we were going to have a summer vacation this year. We're saving for a trip to visit the States this Christmas out of our piddling salary and a jaunt to the coast just didn't seem to be in the cards. Then, our friends, Jeff and Kate, mentioned that we could stay for free at their uncle's house on the coast if we drove them down in our truck. The deal was struck, and here we are—enjoying warm waters and quick sprints out of the rain (no small feat with two little boys, beach toys, towels, bags, car seats, etc.!).

A few minutes ago, our hosts offered to let me check my email, and I declined. I was tempted for sure. There's book business happening and RVA school affairs and family/friends communication to be read/written. Normal life is going on, even through these summer months, but I made myself say no. I'm trying to make this holiday be filled with holy days.

Hold on. I'm not trying to equate us resting with the Dalai Lama on a mountain top or the Pope in the pulpit on Easter Sunday. No. Holy days don't have to mean that the Earth stops spinning and admires how wrinkle-free your soul is.

Holy days are simply holidays, and holidays—if you're not up on the British (and thus Kenyan) lingo—are essentially vacations. Originally, Western holidays were designated by the church calendar—those were the days people took off, went to church, and celebrated with family. Nowadays, the word applies to any time off from work, whether it be for spring break, a national observance, or simply a well-needed break once a year.

As a language lover, I like the word holiday a lot more than vacation. Vacation comes from the Latin word *vaca*, which means empty. The word vacuum (devoid of molecules) has the same root. A vacation is an empty time—empty calendar, empty mind. Nothingness. Void. Space.

Which label would you rather stick on your favorite time of year? Empty days or holy days?

While the name of the break might not really matter, I think the mindset does. I can look at these days by the ocean—crammed in a tiny bedroom with my wife and two small sons, buying seafood from harried fishermen, driving over crater-filled roads for hours at a time—as empty days, days of nothingness. Or I can look at them as holy days.

And this brings me to the concept of Sabbath. Rest is mandated from God. Six days of work and all that jazz. And the concept of sabbatical is also in the Bible, where we take days, weeks, months off to rest, reflect, draw nearer to God. Rest is good.

It's hard to get a Sabbath at Rift Valley Academy, especially on Sunday. Monday through Friday is my 9-5 job. Friday night though ushers in my weekend duties—event sponsor, activities chaperone, Sunday school teacher, worship leader, etc. Heather and I attempt to put one big X on our calendar one day a week where we won't be busy, but sometime scribbles get squeezed in the margins and the rest is lost. Some of my fellow staff members claim that if even one student is on campus, they can't truly rest. I understand that feeling.

So here I am. Doing nothing. Empty days. Building sand castles with Micah and reading something other than student essays. Taking naps and watching Asher practice standing on the couch back. Finding flowers for my wife's hair and ignoring my emails. Enjoying God's aquamarine creation. Vacation.

No, no, no.

Holy days.

The last laugh

I thought I'd better let you know how those three problematic situations from last spring resolved themselves, lest you think I were frozen in my former blood-vessel-throbbing, primal-scream-nearing, Adam-Sandler-with-a-golf-club state.

We got our birth certificate in early June, just a day or two shy of four months of waiting for that one document. A few days later I talked with another new father who was taking time off work with their new little girl and who had the time to get the birth certificate himself. He filled out the paperwork on a Tuesday and picked it up on Wednesday. Why it took our Kenyan gopher 120 times longer than it took our missionary friend, we'll never know. Once we got the Kenyan birth certificate, we applied for a passport and a Report of Birth

Abroad certificate from the US government. Those came two weeks later (on the exact day the U.S. government said they would), and Asher is now free to travel as he chooses (with parental approval, of course) to and from the United States at will.

Our second frustration was the crashed hard drive. This story didn't have such a storybook ending. Our desktop computer is up and running in the technical sense of the word, but whatever our "technician" in Nairobi did to it made the computer run twice as slow, erased one hard drive (the one with ALL of our pictures, videos, and documents), and caused our music to sound like Keith Richards passed out with his elbow on the record player.

The last frustration was the seats. I found someone to make extra seats for the back of our SUV (and thus increase its functionality). When I showed up to have them installed, it turned out that they were an old brown pair (our interior is grey). After searching for over six months, I didn't care. They could've told me that they planned on amputating my arm and turning it into the seat cushion, and I likely would've agreed. Despite the poor quality of the seats and the installation, they proceeded to charge me more than the original quote. I politely asked the "service manager" (both words are ironic at this place of business) to at least give me the quoted price, and I showed her the proposed bill that I'd been given. She admitted that something needed to be done, went to talk it over with her employee, and came back with a new receipt. The new price? Eight dollars *more* than the previous price. She said she found a mistake in his original billing and actually couldn't reduce the price but had to add more on to the bill.

As I left that afternoon, she smiled and asked, "You're not happy?" not understanding why poor service, poor workmanship, poor communication, poor business, and poor value would make someone upset.

I wanted to scream a primordial "Arghh!!!" from the bowels of my missionary angst. I wanted to tell this manager that her incompetence symbolized the trace defects of an entire economy struggling to advance in the world marketplace. I wanted to childishly proclaim that I was packing up my things and going home.

But I didn't.

I simply smiled, got into my vehicle, said, "No, I'm not happy," and drove to my rural Kenyan home.

FALL

Lessons for Lasting
Health

Job 2:4
"'Skin for skin!' Satan replied. 'A man will give all he has for his own life. But stretch out your hand and strike his flesh and bones, and he will surely curse you to your face.'"

Early last week, a violent stomach virus hit our campus so intensely that it had all the earmarkings of food poisoning and not a viral attack. Student Health looked into it, along with the cafeteria staff, and determined that it was indeed a virus which caused the beds in our school infirmary to fill up.

Because we're a boarding school where all the staff and students live on the campus together and really don't leave for three months at a time, viruses like this have a way of spreading rampantly. Just three weeks ago a wave of strep throat swept through (and it still hasn't died), and early last week Micah was one of its victims. I don't have exact numbers, but it's not uncommon for 15% of our campus to pick up the exact strain of each mini-epidemic that sweeps through during a school term.

The violent stomach virus got a hold of us last night— all four of us, all at once. While Heather and I started to feel squeamish shortly after dinner, Micah was the first one to vomit, right around 11 o'clock. The clean-up of his mess—all over his bed, comforter, pillows, and him—woke up brother Asher from his slumber. Then, I chucked cookies and had diarrhea as well, but there was more to come.

I probably couldn't have slept even if Asher had gone back to sleep, but of course he didn't. Heather couldn't even sleep, and she's the Rip Van Winkle in our marriage. So at 2 a.m., I quit trying and woke up to watch a football game on DVD with Asher (he loves to watch football when he has insomnia—pretty cool baby). Just before Penn State lost for the ninth straight time to Michigan, Asher became the third family victim to throw up. About a half hour later, he was sufficiently tired (and probably frustrated from Penn State giving away the game) to go to sleep.

After I put him down and went back to bed with my suffering wife, Micah began screaming with stomach cramps. I gave him a bit of juice and some Motrin, and it must have eased his pain until morning.

Heather and I think we finally dozed off around 4 a.m., after four encore performances in the loo for me and six hours of fetal-position-huddling for her. We slept a solid three hours until we had to call our principal and explain our night and why we'd need substitutes for class today. (Without substitute teachers on campus, sick days are a royal inconvenience for everyone.)

How exactly did we come down with this? Perhaps a hundred different ways. We all rub shoulders with many who were sick. But most likely, it was through our friend Allyson.

Allyson works in the guidance office (in addition to being a fabulous dorm mother) and handles dozens of college applications a day while meeting with their submitters. She felt fine on Saturday when we drove to Nairobi with her and husband Todd for my junior high girls basketball game and supply shopping. That night, however, she came down with the bug and spent all day Sunday incapacitated, a prisoner to the throne.

Approximately 48 hours later, the Murphy clan was also taken hostage. All four of us, all on the same night. Who knows if we spread it to anyone else during our teaching yesterday or our department meetings? Time will tell. It's highly likely though when living inside a germ bubble.

But our health threats aren't just inside the bubble. There are plenty of issues outside of our campus as well; Africa is infamous for disease and pestilence.

Missionaries around the world struggle with the unique illnesses found in foreign countries. A hundred years ago, missionaries used a wooden box to ship their belongings to their countries of service. These storage containers were coffin-sized because missions work was deadly. Our medical knowledge and treatments are better today, but there is still great risk.

Intestinal problems are the number one problem that missionaries face. We often joke that there are two kinds of missionaries—those that know they have an internal parasite and those that don't know they have a parasite. Different foods, inconsistent levels of sanitation, and unclean water in Third World settings create a higher susceptibility for illnesses among missionaries. And then there are respiratory and dermatological illnesses, which may last for just a spell or may stick around longer. Often we're faced with attacks on multiple bodily systems at once.

Of course, there are other epidemics to contend with. While HIV/AIDS has trouble finding its way into missionary circles (for obvious reasons), other notorious illnesses, like typhoid, yellow fever, cholera, tuberculosis, and malaria, too frequently wreak havoc on missionary families. My eldest son and I both have had two bouts with malaria, his first case putting him in the hospital.

Maybe the weirdest thing about health care in Third World countries is there can be sicknesses that are bogeys. Tests and multiple examinations will reveal no clear diagnosis. Yet, a human being is laid low—perhaps even permanently damaged—because of some phantom illness. Such was the tragic case of Ben—a missionary kid whose heart was damaged early in his teenage years by a high tropical fever and later mortally failed him as a college sophomore. And then there was our co-worker Karen, sick for over a year without diagnosis or remedy. Whatever it was, she did finally recover. My buddy Dave had to leave the mission field because of intestinal problems that wiped him out for months. Within days of his return to Arizona, he was 100% again.

The point of my mini-lecture on sickness in missions work is that our personal health is a cost we must consider when signing up. Health problems aren't exclusive to Africa or to the Third World. I often mention the scary story of my nephew Christian who nearly died from multiple infections as a two-month-old in San Diego to prove that our lives and the lives of our children are always in the Lord's hands, wherever we live. But, you do increase your risk factor when you enter a Third World area.

Everything possible must be done to maintain healthy lifestyles and every precaution should be made to ward off those dangerous invaders that can attack us on foreign soil. But we shouldn't be surprised when we're afflicted, and we shouldn't ignore who might be behind the illness.

In the story of Job, God allows Satan to strike Job's possessions and family. Satan intends for the loss to cause Job to withdraw his worship of the Lord. It doesn't. And so the devil pulls out his last card—illness. God, again, permits Satan to infect Job with sickness but forbids him from killing the man. Satan is sure that this final tactic will work.

It was a good plan then, and it's a good plan today. It's hard to translate a Bible when you're suffering from piercing migraines. Building relationships among nationals isn't easy when you barely have the energy to get out of bed. One will struggle to dig wells in the relentless sun when diarrhea has sapped every nutrient and fluid from his body. It's tough to preach a coherent sermon with your head on fire from a fever of 103 for a week straight.

These are the challenges we might face. These are the challenges that might diminish our effectiveness for periods of time. These are the challenges that might steal us away from the mission field. These are the challenges that might sway us to even curse God, as Job's wife suggested he do.

However, these challenges are not larger than our God. If God allows sickness or illness or even death to come into our families, then he will also give us the strength to praise him through it. Somehow, despite all of Job's suffering, the Bible says that this troubled man "did not sin in all he said."

Our highest form of worship is to hold nothing back from God—not our personal well-being, not our children's well-being. Nothing. We offer our everything up to him because he gave everything he could give—the very health and life of his only begotten Son on the cross—for us. He's earned the right to be Lord of even our health.

Stories of Living

The stories from this fall are more about mental health than physical health. We moved to Kenya about 30 months ago, and although we had a few visitors, we sorely needed a boost in morale. We planned a trip to Pennsylvania and San Diego during our school's Christmas holiday, and it was a crazy whirlwind trip that included not only the holidays, thirty-thousand miles of travel, and reunions with hundreds of family and friends, but also a wedding, meeting my nephew and brother-in-law for the first time, and introducing our baby son Asher to his American family. Here are a few highlights of our dramatic re-entry to Western culture after two and a half years in Africa.

The quest for donut

On our first morning in San Diego, I loaded my young offspring into the family transport and embarked on an American rite of passage, a journey of heroic proportions, a manly quest like no other. We went to buy donuts.

Way back in the year 2005, a wonderful land of sugar and lard could be found every few miles in San Diego. The fairytale world was called Krispy Kreme. So naturally, I took my little man down the yellow-lined road to see the wonderful wizard of hot donuts. To my great dismay, I found that the glucose-glazed goodies were now polysaturated poultry patties. My Krispy Kreme store was now Chik-Fil-A. I'd use that information to my advantage later, when I was in the mood for greasy chicken and sugar-ladened tea, but it didn't help me that morning.

Unfulfilled but undeterred, we proceeded to the grocery store across the street. But here is where my mentorship of my son began to fall apart. The vast expanses of an American grocery store made me quickly realize that my autopilot function was gone. I had to think long and hard about how to get the thing I knew I could certainly get here. Donuts, donuts, donuts. Where were they?

Bakery, I thought. I scanned the boxes of baked goods—cakes, muffins, rolls, but no donuts. I wandered around some more until I finally broke down and asked. They were hidden on a small set of shelves behind some bags of bagels. I allowed Micah to pick out a colorful sprinkled one, I got Heather an old fashioned cake donut, and I settled on a disappointing, non-Krispy Kreme chocolate iced. Milk was next on the list.

However, a funny thing happened on the way to the milk aisle. We found a row of boxed and bagged donut varieties. You know, the kinds that could survive a nuclear winter with only slight taste alteration. What to do, what to do? It hadn't dawned on me that there would be more than one area in a store with donuts. We found a much better option there, and now I had to do something which I imagine has never been done in the sanitary history of Ralph's grocery store: I returned to the donut shelves and placed (using the same sterile wax sheets as before) the donuts back in their nice, neat spots, opting for the cheaper donuts.

Back to the milk aisle. We grabbed our milk and headed for the check out. Before we got more than 20 feet though, we came across a table display filled with an even more alluring selection of donuts. These were the in-betweeners, the not-quite-fresh but only moderately fire retardant. The $1.99 sticker was the clincher, and so we had to return a second selection back to their original spot. At this point, I'd been in the store nearly 10 minutes, dragging my wide-eyed three-year-old through the aisles of glimmering fruits and colorful cans.

Since the store was fairly empty, I guess my aimless traipsing caught at least one person's attention. As my box of donuts and jug of milk rode the black treadmill toward the red lasers, the lady asked, "Are you from out-of-town?" I guess a normal San Diegan would have known exactly how many different selections of donuts were available at any given supermarket and wouldn't have taken nearly a quarter of an hour to select two items.

They smiled with relief when I said, "Yes, I live in Kenya." There was a reason why I couldn't procure donuts within a reasonable time frame. I was a foreigner.

The curse of row 13

To quote Michael Scott of *The Office*: "I'm not superstitious, but I'm a little stitious." What happened to us the day we sat in row 13 of an airplane made me more than just a little stitious.

We had our second day of travel on Tuesday (our first started on Thanksgiving night), and it didn't go very well. It was only from California to Pennsylvania. It should've gone very well when you stack it up next to our flight from Kenya to California. To California from Africa? 43 hours of travel time, door to door. To PA from California? A measly five hours in the air. There should be no problem. When we came back to America, Heather lost $40 worth of beauty supplies through US security, I spilled a can of powder baby formula on the airport floor (and inside my laptop computer), we missed our flight in

Washington Dulles Airport by five minutes, and our luggage was all delayed (but not lost) coming to California. A lot went wrong on that grueling flight, but it wasn't as bad as Tuesday. What happened on Tuesday was enough to make anyone a little stitious.

We awoke at 5 a.m. and loaded up three vehicles to drive from Julian (an hour east of San Diego) to the airport. On the way, we needed to drop off our friends' car at their house, so I drove Zac and Shelbi's car, Heather drove her mom's car with our two boys in the back, and Heather's dad drove his truck filled with our luggage. As we caravaned down the hill, it was a frigid morning and still dark. Although there hadn't been precipitation in a few days, the previous week's snow was still melting on various hillsides. I drove rather slowly, both because we were traveling together and because the roads were very winding for a dark morning. About fifteen minutes into the journey, I hit a patch of black ice on a curve. I skidded for a few seconds, regained control, and continued on. A bit shocked, I reached for my phone to try to warn Heather, wanting to somehow let her know to be careful. I now wished I had simply stopped around the bend so my imminent lights would have been a caution sign for her.

She was far too close behind me to call and for her to answer, and when I realized this, I then slowed down and waited for her headlights to appear, hoping that she'd made it through successfully.

I waited. I waited. I waited until there was no possible way that something bad hadn't happened. I began to pray and I turned the car around in the middle of the small road. I headed back the 150 yards around the corner, unsure of what I'd find. Before I could go 50 yards, three cars with blinkers on drove past me—Heather, her dad, and another car. I breathed a sigh of relief. They seemed to be okay, but why the delay?

After turning around again, I found our two cars pulled over and found out that Heather had fishtailed, slid nearly off the left side of the road, slid 180 degrees in the other direction, and slammed into a bank head on. Everyone was okay (although Mom's chronic back pain was aggravated by the jolt), but the front bumper was cracked and a fluid was pouring out of the front of the engine. We decided that the car shouldn't be driven any more but we still needed to get to the airport ASAP. Heather's mom suggested that we return the borrowed car later in the day, leave the wrecked car by the road, and proceed to the airport. We had lost 15 minutes and didn't have much time to spare.

Once we got to the airport, we parked the borrowed car in the airport parking and went to unload Dad's truck curbside. With the truck idling and Heather tending to our two boys, Mom watched the truck and the luggage while a suspicious man lurked vaguely around the area. With everyone emotional frazzled and frantically checking in for our flight (now just 45 minutes away), the man somehow went unnoticed as he grabbed Mom's digital camera.

No one realized it until we all stopped outside of the security checkpoint to say our goodbye that would last the next two years. Mom was terrified as she went to grab her camera to take one last farewell picture. The thief's face immediately came to mind and she was convinced he had taken it. While we tried to propose other positive scenarios, she *knew*. The camera had been stolen and, along with it, her digital memories of our long-awaited visit.

The goodbye was now punctuated with the uncertain future of the car (How badly was it damaged? How would Mom and Dad accomplish the deliveries and repairs later in the day?) and the trauma of theft. To make matters worse, the clock was ticking and our plane left in 25 minutes.

The security checkpoint offered no brevity. We unloaded the contents of two carry-ons and a diaper bag into the trays (filling 18 trays total), and we stripped the winter coats and shoes off of our "extreme-threat-to-national-security" sons. To make matters even worse, they took our suitcases aside for further examination, callous to the fact that we were about to miss our flight.

Heather ran ahead once the first bag was done, and she held the gate open for Micah and me. But since the flight was full, they wouldn't let us take our carry-ons (the very carry-ons which kept us for 15 minutes at security) on board with us. They had to be checked with the other baggage, and so we helplessly watched our digital camera, donated laptops, baby monitor, and alarm clock be taken away to the savage underbelly of the aircraft. Our stroller was checked too. (A stroller we would find broken when we arrived in Washington Dulles.)

Feeling stripped of our possessions and stripped of our emotions, we sidled our way down the aisles and past the angry eyes of the earlier-arriving passengers to our seats. Seats A, B, and C. And the row?

Row 13. Yes, I'm a little stitious too, Michael Scott.

The few positives that came out of this story were that we made our flight, we got all of our luggage in Dulles, and we were reunited with my parents at the airport. We also found out that the only interior damage to the car was the windshield wiper fluid pipe. The bumper would need to be replaced, but it was a relief that no serious damage had happened inside the car.

Oh how we long for the days of cramped seats, bad airplane food, and simple jet lag. Maybe our 43 hours of travel back to East Africa would go better than our five hours of travel to Pennsylvania, I say as I knock on wood and throw some salt over my shoulder.

The next season—winter—will begin with the conclusion of this story. From our whirlwind tour, there was a great lesson to be learned about grieving and the need for prayer.

WINTER

Lessons for Lasting
Prayer

Psalm 109:21-22
"But you, O Sovereign Lord, deal well with me for your name's sake; out of the goodness of your love, deliver me. For I am poor and needy, and my heart is wounded within me."

From Monday night until Tuesday night of our December travels, the Murphy Four experienced what could be called a microcosm of the entire missionary life. "Leaving and grieving" is the catch phrase for the emotional state of chaos in which missionaries and missionary kids find themselves. Our loved ones are scattered around the world, and whenever we leave one set, we find ourselves uprooted and traveling to another, only to be uprooted again. While everyone (missionary or not) feels loss and loneliness and separation from loved ones in one way or another, missionaries go through this in an exaggerated way. All of our relationships are spread across the world, and we spend exponentially more time away from our loved ones than the general population. We're constantly "leaving" someone, and so we're perpetually in a state of "grieving."

I'll start with Monday night, 6 p.m. Pacific time.[1] We celebrated my father-in-law's birthday at Heather's brother's

---

[1] Our December trip technically straddled the seasons fall and winter; hence, you'll find connections between the last chapter and this one. Forgive me for any confusion.

house. The four grandkids romped around the house, the adults enjoyed watching the kids and conversing, we ate some amazing Mexican food (courtesy of my sister-in-law), and we opened some early Christmas presents in addition to Dad's birthday gift. At the end of the night, we said goodbye to Jason and Catherine, Christian and Tierra—not for the night but for the next two years. My nephew's life will double in that time period, and my niece will learn how to read for real (she story-tells while looking at pictures now, fooling my son into thinking she is actually reading). A lot of life will be missed while we're away.

Fast-forward to Tuesday morning—7 a.m. Pacific time. This is the story "The curse of row 13" from last fall. Even without all of the complexities of that traumatic morning, you can imagine grandparents having to say goodbye to half of their grandchildren for the next 24 months. Standing in Terminal 1 at San Diego International Airport brought back horrible memories of our first goodbye from them in June 2005. Heather had never moved away from home before, and her parents had never had a heartbreak like this either. As the husband, the son-in-law, and the man responsible for this move, I felt awful as well, as if somehow I were the one (and not the Lord) who had led us to this life. Luckily, this Tuesday's goodbye was far less difficult, for it wouldn't be an indefinite amount of time until we met again and we'd already been through separation before. These waters weren't unchartered. But the sea was still rough.

After four and a half hours of decompressing on the airplane, we were transported magically to another emotional country—elation. 4 p.m. Eastern time. Waiting outside of baggage claim at Washington Dulles were my dad, step-dad, and uncle—all who had never met Asher and all of whom I hadn't seen in two and a half years. Of course, my mom was there too hugging Micah first of all, but we'd seen her a mere nine months earlier. (All grandmothers out there will note the sarcasm in the word "mere" I'm sure.)

9 p.m. Eastern time. Once we arrived back at my parents' house, my sister and her fiancé came over to see us. She's getting married on Friday, and I'd never even met Clint. It was a joy to meet this fella I'd be calling brother in the next few days, and there was also the joy in seeing her belly with a baby in it. I told her that the surreal feeling of seeing her with a rounded belly was akin to seeing Arnold Schwarzenegger pregnant in *Junior*. I don't think she liked the comparison.

In 24 hours, we had experienced painful goodbyes and mountain highs, tears of sorrow and tears of joy, grieving and rejoicing. This in a nutshell is the emotional life of a missionary family. Not all days may be as intense as this Monday-Tuesday stretch, but every day possesses these emotions. We're joyous to be doing what God wants us to do in Africa; we love the people—of all races, nationalities, and ages—whom we live with. But we long and miss and grieve for those back home. And that's the tension that's more than just a 24-hour phenomenon.

And that's also the tension that brings me to this season's lesson. Prayer. It's crucial to the Christian's life in so many ways, but I'll emphasize three of the most significant.

Prayer is essential for the emotional well-being of a missionary. We need people praying for all of the complex emotions we deal with as we "leave and grieve" on a daily basis. At the very same moment, we are both struggling and striving—struggling with sorrow for loved ones back home and striving to forge new relationships in a foreign land. Both fights are tough ones, but when they occur simultaneously, the battle becomes epic. Prayer is a huge weapon for protecting the heart of a missionary.

Prayer is also crucial for the spiritual work of a missionary. When I stepped out in faith to leave my family, to take my wife from her home, and to become a full-time minister for Christ abroad, I put a huge target on my back. Satan would love to defeat me—relationally, emotionally, or spiritually—any way he can. Satan will try to stop the work I do and will attempt to defeat the spiritual foundations I lay. Prayer protects the ministry of a missionary, for God's glory.

Prayer also protects the physical lives of missionaries. As I mentioned in the lesson from last fall regarding health, Satan uses sicknesses to sack us. Sometimes he even goes a step further—murder. While martyrdom certainly has a sacred and mysterious place in the growth of God's kingdom on earth, we should pray for physical protection from harm. As you'll read in this season's stories, a missionary can go from stability and safety in their host country to chaos and genocide in the time it takes to fire a single gun or to cast a ballot. Prayer is needed to preserve the lives of missionaries in foreign fields.

Living in a cross-cultural setting often gives missionaries an active sense of how "poor and needy" they are, which is also how the writer of Psalm 109 refers to himself. And with the writer, we need to constantly have on our lips the cry of "Deliver me!" Deliver me from the emotional turmoil of "leaving and grieving!" Deliver me from the spiritual attacks of Satan on my ministry! Deliver me from physical harm so I can serve you in this difficult land! Without those cries, we don't stand a chance.

Stories of Living

Our busy but enjoyable trip to the United States ended in a worrisome way. Days before we were scheduled to return to Kenya, the country held its presidential elections. The early reports favored the challenger, Raila Odinga, and celebrations began prematurely among his supporters. The official announcement took longer than expected, and when the government declared that the incumbent president, Mwai Kibaki, had retained his post, violence erupted. By the time we were ready to fly, over 200 deaths had been confirmed, and each new story sounded less hopeful. While we were waiting at the Washington airport, the TVs reported that fifty were dead in a church burning. Hence, our stories for this season will frequently mention the need for prayer, but I also will tell some tales of normal life in Africa.

News from the ground

Our flight arrived safely on Wednesday evening. The plane was only about two-thirds full coming into Nairobi, but we were reassured to see so many people still traveling, many of them tourists. Once we got through customs, we retrieved all but one lost bag. Everything seemed business as usual in the airport, except for the extra police and military all over. The city looked eerily empty as we drove to the guest house for missionaries in Nairobi. The next morning, Jeff and Todd, two friends who risked themselves to drive into the unstable city, picked us up at dawn (in order to avoid a volatile public rally scheduled for late that morning). We arrived safely and completely intact (minus the one suitcase which showed up the next week) at Kijabe at 9 a.m. For the rest of the news, I'll break things down into political and personal.

Political—I only know a skeletal version of the events, but this is what I've learned since being here. Shortly after the vote, reports were so strongly in favor of the challenger that his supporters (consisting of members of the minority tribes in Kenya) began to celebrate in the streets. When the shocking final tally favored the incumbent, the minorities erupted. The incumbent is of the majority tribe (Kikuyu) in the nation, but that majority is only around 25% of Kenya's population. Although tribal feuds exist between all of the tribes, the president's tribe has long been despised because of its dominance. This "stolen election" has given the rest of the country reason to attack. While the situation is still volatile, the whole country is not burning. The rally which was supposed to happen for the challenger yesterday in Nairobi never got off the ground, and so now we're in a holding pattern—with an unofficial president who has not been acknowledged by the rest of the world and a country who won't rest until there is justice.

Personal—We enjoyed our visit so thoroughly in the US that I really didn't look forward to coming back to Rift Valley Academy, and that was before this post-election chaos hit. The last six days now have been not only exhaustingly busy with logistics of travel preparation and actual travel, but the ever-looming decision—*do we really want to fly* into *a situation like this?*—also weighing heavily. But arriving safely to school was a great joy. We spent the day unpacking and visiting with friends and colleagues on campus. RVA has just announced that school will be delayed another two weeks to allow for the political situation to stabilize and to ensure safer travel for our students, so we'll have ample time to readjust.

Thine is the kingdom...

Church on Sunday was a moving experience. Although there has been no violence here in Kijabe, and there is really no foreseeable threat, the hearts of those worshiping were very somber. Even though most (if not all) of the congregants weren't personally touched by the unrest, most (if not all) knew someone who had been burned out of their home or had been beaten or had been robbed or even killed. Their families were affected, and the instability felt nation-wide hurt the people to their core. The future of Kenya and of the Kikuyu population was very much in danger.

As we sang the songs to begin the service, the heart of the Gospel broke through in a new way to me. We sang "and your kingdom will not pass away" with great hope, despite the possibility that the current kingdom in which we live could pass away. We sang "my life is in you, Lord" with minds open to the possibility that our days of life on earth could be numbered. And then to close, we sang "my comfort, my shelter, tower of refuge and strength" with hearts so in need of God's strong arms to care for us.

As I watched eighty Kenyan children walk back the aisles for their children's church, I looked into each face and prayed God would "deliver us from evil. For thine is the kingdom, the power, and the glory, forever and ever."

I've been in Kenya two and a half years, but never has the country been in such an insecure state. And coming from the States, where we haven't had a military attack on mainland in about two hundred years, I'd never felt grave danger while living there. So, the promises of God had all new meaning to me as I sat on the wooden bench Sunday. Trusting God for everything, even my very life, was a new experience, yet the word of God and the songs we sang affirmed that he's very much the God of chaos and strife.

If you've read my writings before, you know I tend to be quite dramatic, and this time is no exception. My life is not in danger. This country is not likely to fall apart. Wicked men will not have the final say here. But the people of Kenya are deeply hurting, and the point I'm trying to make is that the Good News is so, so good for millions across the globe—in Pakistan, in the Middle East, in the Philippines, in South Africa, in Haiti. In the States, things are so good for many people (relatively speaking) that it's easy to only see God's power in the realm of new jobs and the flu and Power Ball numbers. I don't deny the presence of God in those things as well—He's glad to be the God of every little hair on our heads—but it's so awe-inspiring to sense Him as the God of comfort during tumultuous days and life-and-death events.

Political update

A relatively peaceful week in Kenya brought normalcy back to life in Nairobi. City stability goes a long way towards national financial stability and international standing. On our two trips this week (one for food/supplies and one for two new tires) there was nothing out of the ordinary in the city. This is good news.

However, Kenya is much more than large cities. The greatest problems, and probably the ones which will take many years to resolve, lie in the rural areas. In the past century, tribal lines have blurred throughout the country, meaning that no single community is 100% homogenous. Since Kikuyu is the largest tribe, there are more Kikuyu spread throughout Kenya than any other, and when the Kikuyu president was controversially announced the winner of the election, the other tribes took out their anger on the closest Kikuyu. Some examples? There was a church burning (which didn't happen to worshippers, but to women and children hiding in the church from rioters). On the highway near us, a vehicle drove through roadside celebrations of Kikuyus, killing nine. Over 3,000 refugees assembled in the town below us. All had been burned out of their homes, physically assaulted, or had felt threatened.

This kind of violence and threatening behavior has brought about the biggest problem in Kenya today—IDP's, or internally displaced peoples. The country is now littered with tens of thousands of scarred refugees. My language helper Bonface [sic] had ten people living in the living room of his one bedroom house. Thousands of others wait in lines all day for soup from the Red Cross while living in the organization's tented shelters. And what are these people to do while they are displaced? Their livelihoods exist in some other place. So they sit. And wait. Hungry. Grieving.

The hope of the internally displaced people ultimately rests in the government's resolution. Tuesday is the day the new parliament meets for the first time. Parliament is dominated by the presidential challenger's party, so sparks could fly. Then, on Wednesday, Thursday, and Friday protests have been arranged in towns throughout Kenya. While the government easily suppressed last week's rallies in the capital city, maintaining peace in dozens of cities could be a challenge.

Serious mud

I awoke yesterday morning at 5:30 to head to the airport to pick up students for the belated start to our school year. Some of the kids had been waiting there since 5 a.m., but we don't leave Kijabe until there's a bit of daylight for safety reasons.

Normally, a trip to and from town to pick up students consists of zero calls between the driver and school supervisors. In light of the situation here, I sent four text messages and made five phone calls to different people between 6 a.m. and 11 a.m. All of the reports were positive; there were no hot spots on our route yesterday. But we must be careful at a time like this. The van was filled with ten kids, ages 10 through 18, from Uganda, Sudan, and Cameroon.

Like I said, travel went very smoothly all around yesterday. Probably the most dangerous part of my journey was my footwear. Outside the airport, I remembered to lock the back hatch to secure the kids' luggage. The place where I got out of the van was muddy with this thick red clay. I tried to knock the mud off on the side of the van, but that was a joke. This mud was serious. It was the E.F. Hutton of mud, the Jonathan Edwards, the Vince Lombardi. I found myself mired in John Wayne mud. Actually, now that I think about it, the word "mud" probably didn't even do this stuff justice. Imagine if an elephant could chew gum and then spit it out by the side of the road. Then, envision my shoes stepping in this massive piece of gum. You know how relentless one little piece of gum is on the soles of your shoes; multiply that times 200. That's a better description. Anyway, driving home with this stuff on my shoes was a chore, constantly moving my feet off the gear pedal, brake, and accelerator to prevent permanent cohesion. I would've pulled over at a gas station and washed it off with a hose if I'd felt more comfortable in the city right now. Instead, I drove the two hours home with elephant gum on my shoes— the most dangerous part of my journey bringing students back to campus yesterday.

Belated celebrations

We celebrated Asher's first birthday a few days late this year. A room full of school friends helped him and us commemorate the event. He wasn't too into the cake, but he loved crawling after the balloons. Gifts from grandparents in the

U.S. (shipped back in our suitcases from December) and a Cookie Monster cake made by mommy highlighted the evening.

Kenya is celebrating tonight as well. A picture in today's paper featured Kibaki and Odinga shaking hands and smiling. After so much animosity between these two men, their political parties, and their tribes, it's confusing to see them so cordial. I wish I could say I felt happy and relieved; I hope that Kenyans everywhere feel happy and relieved. I hope this is the real deal. Let the healing begin. Let the new government begin to work in a democratic fashion. Let justice and law return to the country. Let it be, Lord.

Those are so much more than words. The pain runs so deep here. Over 900 reported dead from the violence. An estimated one million IDP's. The destruction of two months will take lifetimes to rebuild.

Our students led a chapel service on Wednesday in which six upperclassmen Kenyan boys shared their testimonies on how the violence and unrest affected them personally. One boy's father lost his business to fire and theft. Another boy spoke of his terror living as minority tribe member in the midst of bloodshed and mayhem. The last boy who spoke, the point guard on our varsity basketball team, shared why he was a week late coming back to school. He was cleaning the gunshot wounds of his mother. She survived and is doing fine, but this certainly explained why he didn't return on time. His wounds are healing too—slash marks from machetes, which thankfully did not prove fatal.

The smiles on those politicians' faces had best be sincere. Their words and promises today had best be true. There has been enough pain.

SPRING

Lessons for Lasting
Generosity

Haggai 1:9
"You expected much, but see, it turned out to be little. What you brought home, I blew away. Why?" declares the LORD Almighty. "Because of my house, which remains a ruin, while each of you is busy with his own house."

As I drove down the winding, muddy road to the valley today, I explained to my four-year-old son why we were going to give food and to share God's Word with two dozen HIV/AIDS infected women and their children. I quoted Jesus' Golden Rule ("Do unto others what you would have them do unto you") and let his four-year-old logic (which quite often baffles and infuriates me) do the rest.

If you were sick, Micah, what would you want someone to do for you?

"Make me feel better," he said.

If you were hungry and poor, what would you want someone to do for you?

"Give me some food," Micah said.

If you were sad and lonely? "Cheer me up," he said.

Our conversation didn't go any deeper than that. And it didn't need to. He got it. He didn't need a WWJD? bracelet on his wrist to figure out what Jesus would do. Sometimes, it's simple.

And so we sat in this 15x60 feet room, with around 70 women and children, over half of whom will die in the next decade from AIDS. Micah made faces at the little boys and girls who were staring at us, and they took turns playfully poking back and forth. I shared Romans 8:28[1] with the joyful women (yes, they were joyful to be receiving food and assistance on this day) and then sat back down on my wobbly wooden bench.

But the thought that kept running through my mind was, "What if this were me?" What if I or my spouse or parent had made some sinful choices out of poverty or hopelessness and had contracted AIDS? Or what if I were raped or molested, and now my future is illness and doom and death? What would I hope for? Desire? Wish?

And then I thought about Micah and these kids he was playing with. What if Micah were born with AIDS? What if his life were destined for suffering from day one? What would be my prayer as a parent? What would I cry out to God every night, with every ounce of strength on Micah's behalf?

Jesus said, "Do unto others what you would have them do unto you." What would I want others to do to me if I were suffering from HIV, if my child were dying from AIDS?

It's not really hard to find the answers if you're willing to honestly put yourself in someone else's shoes. And the answer almost always lies in giving somehow. Time. Money. Prayers. Generosity is the key to a life of love. If we're supposed to "do unto others," well, generosity is what love does.

The ironic thing about missionaries is that we volunteer ourselves to be generous. We sign on to a life where we leave it all behind, but we can't go anywhere unless others are generous. Without the financial and prayer support of like-minded people, we're stuck. Our generosity with our lives only goes as far as the generosity of those who send us out.

Because of the pauper lifestyle that most missionaries embrace, we tend to head off to our countries of service believing that we're poor. We're usually a little stingy and

---

[1] "And we know that in all things God works for the good of those who love him, who have been called according to his purpose."

cautious with our finances because, hey, we're surviving off of donations ourselves. It doesn't take too long living in a Third World context to realize we're not poor at all.

Suddenly, our pocket change looks like a treasure chest, and our monthly allotment seems like a gold mine. We start seeing how our excess money, no matter how little, can be a life-giving blessing to those who are truly poor. We start redefining what it means to "need" some material thing and what it means to be wealthy. After a short time, missionaries find themselves giving and giving to the poor around them when, just a short plane ride earlier, we were the ones on the receiving end.

It's not even a conscious choice really. You see a need, you have the means (even if it's just barely) to meet the need, and you do it. It's what you'd want done unto you, right? It seems so logical that even a four year-old could grasp it.

And yet there are Christians out there who don't get it, or feign ignorance. They are busy (like the people God described to Haggai in this lesson's verse) looking after their own homes and their own private kingdoms, while God's house goes neglected. And in the end, God says, these self-centered ones end up with the least of all. They plan for abundance, they expect much, and yet it simply isn't enough. Contentment and satisfaction and joy never comes, all because God's house is neglected.

During Old Testament times, they were speaking of a literal house for God, a temple that needed to be rebuilt. That was an important concept for worship in ancient times. A temple went hand-in-hand with the worship of a deity. Today, I think 1 Corinthians 10:13 helps us understand a more modern application. Paul writes, "Do you not know that your body is a temple of the Holy Spirit, who is in you, whom you have received from God?"

Human beings, those whom God came to redeem, are the chosen dwelling place of the Almighty. He loves each one of us, regardless of where we were born or what color our skin is or how much money we have. And because he loves us, he considers us his temple if we will invite him in.

Now the verses in chapter 1 of Haggai come into clearer focus. There are lives in ruins all around us, temples of the Living God strewn about in wreckage. To rebuild these lives will take time and money and will demand that we stop spending so much time and money on ourselves.

You may enter a life of Christian service thinking you're a generous person. But, I'm willing to bet that along the way you'll find that you can never give enough. And in many ways, that's going to be the best feeling there is.

Stories of Living

This chapter focuses on our "giving" relationships with different Kenyan friends. Relationships in a Western context usually don't involve finances, but in Africa, they almost always involve finances. While this often cheapens the relationship in a Westerner's eyes, it's really just a normal and seamless facet of friendship here. "The love of money" will tell two stories of those relationships gone bad, and "A Heifer for Harriet/Blood, sweat, and tears" will tell of the best possibilities for our financial giving. "Charity or racism?" asks some hard questions about our prejudices as we try to help out those less fortunate.

The love of money

Two tragic stories come from this past week. Last week, a custodian for the elementary building here on campus was caught stealing two bags of concrete from the construction site (Rift Valley Academy is building a new cafeteria) with his friend's car. The construction company had him arrested for a few days, and of course his seven years of employment at our school came to end.

In the shock and aftermath, stories began to surface from many missionaries about loans they had given to this man over the course of the past year. Some of the loans were small (under $50), and some were large (over $100). Some he had begun to pay back; some he was tardy on. All of his loans had come with grace and generosity on part of the missionary. In total, this man had been given and loaned hundreds and hundred of dollars, on top of his making a healthy income in a country where the unemployment rate is about 70%. Everyone felt betrayed, having believed that he was truly needy and that they were really making a difference in his life.

This man's greed went so far that he called another missionary from prison and asked him for another $200 loan, hoping that he hadn't heard about his recent lawlessness.

Even more heartbreaking for us was the news we received of our former nanny. If you read my first book, you know how we employed her for our first 18 months here in Kenya and really felt attached to her and her family. That came to an abrupt end though when we began piecing together a horrible story of lies and theft on her part. Over the course of her employment with us, she stole somewhere between $200 and $700. (Her stealing was so subtle and her access to our "hidden" money so easy that we can't know exactly how much was taken.)

My language helper, Bonface [sic], told me that he saw our former nanny drunk and leaving a local bar with a man other than her husband. And this confirmed the rumors he had heard—she was now a prostitute.

This may seem shocking and mind-boggling and horrific to you. It is to us as well, especially considering the prevalence of AIDS in Africa. But we understand how our former nanny could make choices like this. The following verse from I Timothy 6:9-10 explains it all. "People who want to get rich fall into temptation and a trap and into many foolish and harmful desires that plunge men into ruin and destruction. For the love of money is a root of all kinds of evil. Some people, eager for money, have wandered from the faith and pierced themselves with many griefs."

Our former nanny and the school custodian both enjoyed fellowship in the church, both called themselves "blessed" by God, and both found themselves financially successful in this economic system. But they wanted to get rich. They began to love the things that money could buy more than the One who provides money for our needs. They wandered from the faith and have pierced themselves with many griefs. And for both of them, there will be many more griefs to come if they don't repent.

Our former nanny would rather be a prostitute making extra money than a church leader and an honest working woman. (Ironically, her husband is still gainfully employed by the school so her family *does* have enough!) The custodian would rather be the richest man with the nicest house in his neighborhood than be a respectable, faithful, honest, hard-working provider for his family.

Money is not the root of all evil, but the love of money is. Sadly, these two friends of mine, whom I once called brother and sister, gave tragic examples of the truth of God's Word this week.

A heifer for Harriet

Of all the great things about our trip to the States in December—In-n-Out Burger, Krispy Kreme donuts, family (in no particular order)—getting to see my Aunt Kim and Uncle Chris and their family for the first time in about seven years was a highlight.

When they mentioned that their church in Limerick, PA, participated in the Heifer Project and might be interested in buying a cow for someone in Kenya, I had the perfect someone in mind.

Harriet is a single mother of two kids—a teenage girl and a pre-school boy—and is struggling to support her family in a harsh economy. We employ her a few hours a week watching our sons while we teach, but things are still hard for her.

Before Harriet became a Christian, she was married and living in Kenya's capital, Nairobi. Her life was hard, and she did many things she was ashamed of. In 2003, just after the birth of her son, Harriet decided to follow the Lord Jesus Christ. Her husband was not happy about her decision, and his neglect of the family increased. Although Harriet tried to support her two children and her husband on her own, his drunkenness forced Harriet to make a hard decision for the good of her family. She moved with her two children to an area near Kijabe, which is where some of her relatives lived. Sadly, her husband didn't care.

Harriet does her best to raise her children to obey the Lord, taking them to prayer meetings throughout the week and church on Sundays. The love and salvation of Christ is evident in her daily demeanor, her excellent work, and her grateful testimony.

Buying a cow isn't an everyday American purchase. Beggars don't stand along the side of freeways asking for cows. So, what's the deal with purchasing livestock for the poor?

Much like in biblical times, livestock is a form of wealth in Kenya. But for single parents like Harriet, the focus isn't on accumulating wealth but on survival. Milk is one of their few sources of protein and calcium, so it's a staple of the Kenyan diet. Their own cow would not only save them that daily expense, but it would provide them with more milk than they currently drink. And more milk means healthier children and a healthier Harriet.

But that's not the only benefit a cow would bring for Harriet. The cow would graze around the property where she lives, saving her the work of clearing grass and shrubs. Plus, cow manure is a valuable commodity as fertilizer in this agricultural setting. Harriet could use the manure for her garden and improve her own crops. Any manure that is unneeded can be sold to neighbors for about four dollars a sack.

Well, after hearing Harriet's story, the youth group from my relatives' church sprung to action and raised the whole amount—plus some extra for a shed to house the cow.

Once the money was in, the next task was to find a cow. If Kenya had Wal-Marts, I'm pretty sure they'd sell cows. Since they don't, Harriet needed a few weeks to ask around and find the perfect deal. Once that deal was brokered, it was time to make a home for the cow to come home to.

Because the party can't start in Africa until the cow comes home.

Blood, sweat, and tears

Saturday, our family spent the day helping Harriet build a pen for her forthcoming cow. After a few weeks of planning and preparation, we finally assembled the team to "git-'er-done."

And git-'er-done we did, with a little blood, sweat, and tears.

The first blood (not the *Rambo* movie, mind you) came on Friday night as my Kenyan friend John and I went shopping together in a rented school van. We drove down into a rock quarry, up the hill to a roadside sand mound, and into a town twenty minutes away for lumber, sheet metal, and cement. Right before our last purchase, I sliced open my thumb on the edge of the sheet metal (for the roof of the pen) as we were trying to make room for all of our friendly "advisors" we assembled along the way. John and I picked up four other men who were ready to help us find our next item on the list (for a small tip), and their assistance really was useful. As I stood in a crowded shopping center, dozens of Kenyans gathered around the *mzungu* (white) to watch us negotiate for two bags of cement (price tags don't exist in Kenya…it's all about getting as much as you can). Meanwhile, my sliced finger is gushing blood onto the dirt below me. More embarrassed than in pain, I finally realized what one of our "advisors" was saying to me: "Plaster for five. Plaster for five." Plasters (an English term) are Band-Aids, and he was going to help me by buying me one for five shillings. I popped it on my dirty cut and finished the deal. As we drove away from this scene, I told John about Home Depot and how this experience was a bit different for me. He nodded with saucer eyes and mouth agape.

The next morning Heather, Micah, and I picked up three of our sophomore students at their dorms and our friend John at his house five minutes away. We then joined our "project supervisor" (Harriet's friend) and Harriet's dad at her house for the sweat part. Luckily, it was an overcast, misty day so there wasn't too much sweat to be had. But the job was finished by five o'clock that night, and in the end, Harriet had a fully-functioning cow shed—complete with feeding area, cement floor in the sun, covered mud-area for protection from rain, milking area, and whirlpool/jacuzzi. (Just kidding on that last part.)

The first tears of the day were from Asher as he had to stay home with a babysitter. At fifteen months of age, he's good with a hammer, but we thought we should delay his first construction project until he can balance on a beam from fifteen feet in the air. Maybe next year. The next tears came from our eldest son. He never tired of the work (supplying nails, carrying sticks, moving rocks), but he did find himself in the wrong place once. Four of us were standing under the roofed part of the shed with our backs to the man sawing above us. While we formed almost a complete wall blocking little Micah, one 2x3 board flew off the handsaw and navigated its way through us to his forehead. It was a totally improbable injury. He ended up with a little knot on his head after the tears stopped flowing, but he wanted to get right back to his work.

The only other possible tears of the day probably came from Harriet. You see, the gift she was given cost more than she'd ever be able to afford. With a daughter in high school (only grades 1-8 are free in Kenya) and without a husband to help her, she will be fighting to stay afloat in this economy. But because a group of youth outside of Philadelphia wanted to share Christ's love in a tangible way, she has a better life ahead of her. And that's a good reason for tears of joy.

Charity or racism?

Two events happened in my life last Wednesday that made me examine Western attitudes towards Africa. There are few places to go "out" to eat here in Kijabe. One of them is our local hospital's cafeteria. For my language lesson this week, my helper suggested we work on my mealtime conversation skills. While I waited for him to arrive (he was 30 minutes late and running on Africa time, of course), I tried to study my flash cards but was distracted by an American woman's voice. When I stopped reviewing and actually watched her interact with the Africans around her, I lost my appetite.

She was the only white woman in the group, and she was about twenty years older than the oldest African. Through her annoying permanent smile, she affectionately cuddled up to the people and asked them infantile questions about their food and their feelings and such. The people were obviously uncomfortable, but since this lady was clearly helping them in some way (Did she bring them for check-ups? Did she promise them a free meal?), they were tolerating her personality the best they could. You're not going to brush off someone who could potentially change your life if her wallet is big enough, right?

I felt sick watching her. If I could've magically changed every African person in that cafeteria to a soft, cuddly puppy dog, I think this woman's tone would have been exactly the same. Staring at them, touching them, speaking at them—she seemed to treat them like animals gathered around the feeding dish. It looked more like condescension to me than like charity.

Event #2. That night, after our boys went to sleep, Heather and I watched a DVD of *American Idol* from a year ago (remember, we get our TV shows slightly after the air date). The episode was called "Idol Gives Back," and it featured the usual cast of judges, the six remaining contestants, and a slew of famous entertainers. The focus of their charity for this night was poverty in various American cities and suffering in Africa. The show volleyed between live blockbuster performances and video vignettes of the *Idol* hosts visiting the poor of the world. Most of their "African" segments actually were Kenyan. We recognized the cities and the slums, and of course, we recognized the problems that they documented through our own firsthand experiences.

Raising awareness and raising funds for the poor are causes I love. (I wish it were all done in the name of Jesus, but if it's saving lives, I'm not going to criticize.) It was inspiring to see millions of dollars raised to help. But as I watched the celebrities teleport themselves from Hollywood Blvd. to the slums of Kibera, Kenya, and the FEMA housing of New Orleans, it was hard to stomach this brand of charity.

First off, I had trouble watching these multi-millionaires share the spotlight with these truly afflicted people. Did rubbing shoulders with the poor effect them…move them to tears…change their perspective? Sure. You'd have to be badly programmed robot not to weep as you watch an 18 year-old girl breathing the last breaths of her battle with AIDS. And the cameras got every frown and tear from our television stars. But how easy was it for Seacrest to go back to his $200 dinner entrees and for Cowell to rev up one of his dozen sports cars when he returned from his trip? The disparity between the base lowliness of these orphans, these destitute, and these dying and the glamorous righteousness of these beautiful, rich celebrities was disturbing.

To make matters worse, in my opinion, was the way the cameras and the celebrities used them—as objects of sympathy and as creatures. Rather than speak to these people as human beings equally created beautiful in God's image, they spoke down to them as charity cases. I heard the same (dare I say "racist"?) tones from the old white lady earlier in the day as I was now hearing on this television show.

I don't want to come across as self-righteous. Perhaps I'm too late. I have recordings of some of my first language sessions with my helper, and I hate the tone of voice I used. My first helper wasn't the first black woman I ever talked with, and she wasn't the poorest person I ever talked with. But she was African, and as a new Westerner in this culture, I guess I couldn't help but talk down to her. To view her as different and less and "other." Maybe I still speak like this to my Kenyan friends? I don't know. I pray not.

One of the biggest lessons I've learned—and am still learning—is that one human being is no different from another. Read that again. One human being is no different from another. You may be sick, and I may be healthy. We're no different. I may be poor, and you may be rich. We're no different. You may be brown, and I may be white. You may come from that side of the sea, and I from this side. One human being is no different from another. We're the same.

Shakespeare wrote in *The Merchant of Venice*: "Hath not a Jew eyes? Hath not a Jew hands, organs, dimensions, senses, affections, passions; fed with the same food, hurt with the same weapons, subject to the same diseases, heal'd by the same means, warm'd and cool'd by the same winter and summer, as a Christian is? If you prick us, do we not bleed? If you tickle us, do we not laugh? If you poison us, do we not die?"

Paul wrote in Galatians: "There is no Jew nor Greek, slave nor free, male nor female, for you are all one in Christ Jesus."

And because we're the same, how can I not give to you, help you, speak on your behalf, share with you? Charity is my calling.

But how dare I, in the act of giving and in the process of helping, look down on you as any less than I am! Pride is my true enemy as I attempt to be a generous person. Charity without pride is the only way to give.

Part Three

Summer

Lessons for Lasting
Accuracy

2 Timothy 2:15
"Do your best to present yourself to God as one approved, a workman who does not need to be ashamed and who correctly handles the word of truth."

This lesson is a bit of a stretch for me. You see, I'm not a Bible teacher, and I've had very little formal Bible training. I am a student of the Bible, as all Christians should be, but my knowledge of God's Word is far behind that of most of the missionaries on the field. That said, perhaps this qualifies me more than anyone else to make this next point.

The Gospel we teach and the Gospel we live must both be 100% accurate, as far as we can help it.

Maybe some Christians around the world can fudge on this. You know how it is. Let's say there are three Christian men at your church, and although there are many good and godly things about these men, everyone knows that one has an anger problem, one has a lying problem, and one has more pride than a boardroom full of executives. But they get away with it. There is enough sound biblical teaching within the church and enough good examples of patience, truth, and humility to negate the effect of those ungodly characteristics. The true Gospel still goes out from that church despite the human failings within the members of the church.

In many fields of mission work, such a luxury is not afforded. If you're the first missionary there, you *are* the

Gospel. Your words and actions reflect the God you are unveiling to them. They see you and they are learning about this "Jesus" whom you proclaim. How's that for pressure? Do you notice how I don't distinguish between the Gospel that is preached and the Gospel that is lived? It seems that all cultures in the world, and not just our American one, inherently hate hypocrisy. Tell a national that God is generous as you hoard possessions in your house and give very little, and you will be sending mixed messages. Tell a national that God is love while you shy away from relationships and social events in the community, and you will be living out a different Gospel than you preach. There's a reason that Jesus got so fired up about the Pharisees all the time. Hypocrisy is a truth-killer.

For my friends the Busers, Bible translators and church planters in Papua New Guinea, "correctly handling the word of truth" is of utmost importance. They know the importance of laying a solid and firm foundation as they continue on with their work. They could probably have gone in, shoddily translated a few key verses, got a handful of converts, and then got out. They could be back in the U.S. today bragging about the "church" they started and the "converts" they gained in Papua New Guinea, and no one would be able to challenge them on it. But that's not the way God's Word and God's plan for discipleship thrives.

Instead, they have chosen to learn the language and the culture accurately, and it takes many, many years for that to even begin to happen. In the area of language, how do you translate verses about God "standing at the door and knocking" to a culture without doors to their homes? Without years of word study, you may never learn that the liver, and not the heart, is where emotion and will reside to a particular people group. Culturally, missionaries have to navigate the minefields of syncretism as they go about it. Otherwise, Jesus could be neatly placed on the religious shelf among hundreds of other gods, fully "accepted" into the culture but not fully accepted as Lord and Savior of the people. Syncretism threatens to undermine any attempt to bring a biblical worldview into a culture, and missionaries must constantly be teaching in a way that the differences between God's righteousness and culture's sinfulness[1] are illuminated and not blended together.

An ugly trend I've seen in African Christianity has come from the American "health-and-wealth" gospel. In a nutshell, proponents of this brand of Christianity teach that if you believe in God, you will be healthy and rich. In Kenya, where the average adult makes $1 a day and over 5% of the population suffers from either HIV/AIDS or some other life-threatening disease, you can see the appeal. This false gospel runs amuck at revivals (often funded or led by Westerners) and influences first-time believers and established Christians. In time, you will find these "converts" worshiping money rather than God (as evidenced in theft, illegal prostitution, or drug sales) or going off of antivirals, all because of the erroneous preaching they've heard and accepted.

If our work is to be approved by God, we have to constantly return to Scripture for our teaching. We can't rely on Western Christianity (no matter how "right" we feel it is), and we can't rely on our own common sense. We not only have to live out a life that lines up with the Gospel according to our own understanding, but we have to teach a model of Christian living that makes sense within the culture in which we find ourselves. Again, that takes time and accuracy if it's to be done well.

Scratch that. Living out the Gospel takes time and accuracy if it's to be done at all. This point of accuracy is just that important. If the DNA and destiny of a mighty redwood

---

[1] Not everything about a culture is sinful. Some early missionaries went out with that worldview and did much damage to indigenous cultures while perpetuating a "Western" Christianity that had a skewed foundation. This is an important side note because missionaries are often portrayed as destroyers of culture. Good missions don't involve entirely changing or destroying a culture, but desire to redeem a culture and to allow it to praise God in its own unique way.

begins in a tiny seed, then it is equally essential and far more important that the seeds of truth planted by missionaries be right and true.

Stories of Living

The first story can be connected to this season's lesson as an example of a failure of faith in overcoming worldview. Although Christianity is a key voice in Kenya these days, the tribal violence and civil bloodshed of last winter happened anyway. "Not the good kind of summer camp" tells a beautiful story of healing amidst heartache. "Emergent vs. Reform" chronicles the catch-up work I'm trying to do on American church trends while I'm overseas. My last story in this section—"Neighbor or alien invader?"—asks if the American church has developed an inaccurate belief system about death.

Not the good kind of summer camp

Six months ago, the violence in Kenya was just beginning to subside. The post-election unrest had claimed nearly a thousand lives nationwide and tens of thousands of people were fleeing their homes. Because tribes have blended and migrated through the years, many Kenyan communities had become little melting pots. However, the election of December 2007 divided them, causing neighbor to turn on neighbor.

For most of 2008, these IDP's (internally displaced people) lived in overcrowded Red Cross or UNICEF camps. Eventually, the Kenyan government came through with something to help. For those who had been burned out or physically intimidated out of their homes, the government gave small allotments of money as compensation. The amount was too small to do much and was especially insufficient for buying individual plots of land. However, if individuals pooled their money, they'd be able to buy a plot of land and share it. And that's what they did.

On this patch of land, now called a "camp" for IDP's, each family owns the right to have a small tent on the dusty, barren, dry, windy valley floor. There is no water. No resources. No sanitation. No shade. And this is where thousands of adult Kenyans and their many thousand children will live for an indefinite period of time.

This is the sad part.

But the beautiful part of the story is that Sunday, a group of young Kenyan adults and teenagers in our area, raised money and resources to take down to the IDP camps. Although these people are far from wealthy themselves, they recognize that they have so many more material goods and that they are obligated to share them with those poorer than they. A group of missionaries drove the Kenyans to the camp for their ministry outreach, and we spent Sunday afternoon giving out jugs of water, firewood, bags of grain, clothing, and candy.

It really wasn't much, when you consider how many people were in the camps. But the people were so grateful for the little we were able to give them. And the biggest joy of the day for me was watching Kenyans—whom I usually see on the receiving end of my American, Christian charity—generously giving to those in need because of the compassion God put in their hearts.

Emergent vs. Reform

When we were back in the U.S. in December, I found myself in a sticky situation. While catching up with some friends, I learned that there were two factions that had developed within American Christianity in the three years that I'd been gone. And apparently, one should choose a side for the good of his/her faith. Who knew?

The two sides can be largely grouped as the Emergent Church or the Reform Movement.

Perhaps thirty years ago, the factions would have been liberal Christianity versus conservative Christianity, but I guess some of that "battle" has become irrelevant. "Liberal" denominations have gotten so far away from the kinds of ministries and theology of conservative churches that they're not really on the same playing field anymore. So now, it's as if conservative Christianity—sold-out, born-again believers of the Bible who want to be changed internally and to see change in the world—has turned on itself.

The Emergent side is accused of being theologically relativistic and squishy, of not speaking the hard truth of the Gospel when it comes to sin and hell. The Reform side is accused of spending more time splitting hairs over biblical minutia than reaching out to the lost person of the "post-modern" generation and of not being Jesus's "hands and feet" in a hurting world. Both sides seem to, at times, border on hatred for each other as they throw out their barbs of "heretic" or "Pharisee" at the other. And even when the intensity of the debate isn't as hot, there still seems to be an attitude of "you're for us or against us" coming from each camp.

So I found myself reading more, listening more, and studying more—trying to figure out why my friends had suddenly decided that "mere Christianity" wasn't enough anymore. And I was trying to find out where I should fit in within this controversy. That led me to write an email to Ray, one of my friends and mentors.

My email said:

> "I appreciated your wisdom about the Reform Theology vs. Emergent Church debate during our talk in December. I'm still wrestling with it. I came across an interview with Rob Bell (unofficial Emergent leader) and he talked about all of the venomous attacks he's been getting from Reformers. He basically said—with thousands of people dying from AIDS and poverty and slavery and you-name-it, I don't think it's worth the time to sit around and debate theology and split hairs. What do you think about that? What's more important? A life spent

forming a right theology...or a life spent serving the poor and the suffering?

Ray's response:

"All the important issues in life are found between a tension of opposites. One of the key ideas in my life has been the discovery, through physics, that the answer to these sorts of questions is never with one side or the other. It is absolutely true that "right theology" is important. That is what differentiates Christianity from other religions, cults, and heresies. But it is also absolutely true that at the heart of the Gospel is "God so loved the world" and that we are to be God's hands in a world to ameliorate suffering and pain. Jesus's ministry was mostly to the poor and outcasts. If in the interest of right theology, we sacrifice our love for the Brethren, or the world for that matter, then our theology is useless. If we give all we have in sacrifice to the wrong God, even if we help some people along the way, then our sacrifice is idolatry. We are called to live in a unique balance where love (faith) and reason (efforts) coexist in a unity with the Spirit of God. God's Spirit will help you discern when things are out of balance. In a nutshell, it is never either-or. It is always both. Is an electron a particle or a wave? It is both. Is Jesus a man or God? He is both. Do I have free will or does God determine everything? It is both. Are we saved by grace or works? It is both. That's the short answer. I hope this helps."

It did help. Accuracy and right belief are important; works that flow from truth are also essential. Ray's answer gave me confidence to seek truth rather than a side because that's the side I want to be on. Whether that "answer" is enough to appease either my Emergent friends or my Reform friends, I don't know. I hope it is. We Christians have enough spiritual enemies to fight in this world without turning our guns on ourselves.

Neighbor or alien invader?

I've been sitting on this topic for a while. It's not the cheeriest of subjects, and I fear my North American audience won't be able to relate.

Death and sickness are a way of life in the Third World. Babies die of simple illnesses. Mothers die in childbirth. Diseases like malaria don't discriminate among age or gender. HIV/AIDS plagues the uneducated and the poor. We've seen these things first hand among our Kenyan neighbors and friends.

During our first year or so, I thought it was just an "unlucky" streak, a bad coincidence that people were sick and dying with such frequency around us. Once we got well into our second year, I began to think differently on the subject. I began to see the effects of poverty, poorly trained healthcare providers, and ignorance on the overall lifespan of my African neighbor.

Poverty—A trip to the doctor is expensive, and people don't have health insurance. So, they wait and wait and wait to visit the doctor. Sometimes they wait too long.

Inexperienced healthcare providers—Taken all together, there are few Kenyan doctors (in proportion to the population), and while they have gone through extensive schooling, their preparation and expertise isn't at the level of their Western counterparts. And since lawsuits aren't common here, dare I say that some doctors aren't as careful as they should be?[2]

---

[2] For an example of a hasty diagnosis, take the case of a woman who went to the hospital with a sore throat and was told she should have her thyroid removed and then take medication for the rest of her life. Another doctor correctly treated the strep throat and she felt normal in a few days.

Ignorance—A simple understanding of germs and the way the human body works—the kind of explanation I got in a fifth grade, tenth grade, and freshman year of college health class—would pay off in the long run in fighting disease and death.

These are three huge factors in my opinion, and yet death finds a way to weasel its way into other areas of life. Last week, another death hit the community. A three-year-old boy choked to death on a bottle cap. I don't know all the details, but I can guess. Children are given free reign in the community with older children expected to look after younger children. Although trash does not line the streets, litter is a very common thing. Again, I don't know the whole tragic story, but I'm probably not far off.

Emotionally, when I heard of this death, I went back instantly to last summer, when Daniel—the Kenyan friend with whom I went to Mbooni—lost his one-year-old son to a weeklong illness. Or to last month when a custodian in my classroom building died of a brain hemorrhage. It seems to happen so fast here, and so frequently, leaving us with shock, sadness, and, for me, a study of grief.

When death and sickness live next door, you learn to cope. You get used to their antics. You never become friends with them (ever since the fall of Adam, death has been mankind's enemy), but you learn to accept them. Death is just a part of life.

By contrast, death and sickness hit like a tornado in Western countries. They are foreign and strange and vicious— an unwanted visitor, an aberration. Usually they come with warning—as dark skies presage danger—but even then, we long for the storm to pass and blue skies to resume. And if lightning strikes (in the form of a sudden heart-attack or a car accident like the one that took Steven Curtis Chapman's five-year-old daughter last week), we find ourselves dumbfounded, confused, lost.

Because death and sickness have become "unusual" habits of life for Westerners, we rail against them vehemently. We scream, *Why? It wasn't his time! How could a good God do this?* Our expectation of life is health and longevity, and if anything gets in the way of our God-given right to live comfortably for a seeming eternity here on earth, we throw our fists at the sky and curse whoever is up there. This seems to be our modern worldview, whether we're Christian or not.

So where do these observations lead me? Am I proposing that a world with more needless illness and tragic death is a good thing? Of course not. While I wish Third World poverty could end and fair, equitable healthcare would be available for every man, woman, and child, I know that's not likely. My insight, then, comes for you, my Western reader, and me, your Western narrator.

Since death and sickness are part of the human condition, we'd do well to give thanks to God for all the health around us—ours, our loved ones, our friends—and to accept death and sickness as our common human foe at every turn. Not as some alien invader from outer space crashing our shiny, happy party, but as our wicked neighbor next door who will always be at work and will occasionally have his way with us until Christ returns.

FALL

Lessons for Lasting
Transparency

2 Corinthians 12:9-10
"But he said to me, 'My grace is sufficient for you, for my power is made perfect in weakness.' Therefore I will boast all the more gladly about my weaknesses, so that Christ's power may rest on me."

Brad—the missions pastor at our home church in San Diego—is the guy I always talk to before I do something really stupid. Mildly stupid things I feel at liberty to do on my own, but for the really stupid things, I'd rather get Brad's blessing before going forward.

Before we left for Kenya, I had a hard-nosed business guy grill me at a Bible study about how much money we needed to raise to begin our career as missionaries. He wanted to know where every dollar went, and I had no idea if disclosing that to him (or to anybody else who asked) was a good idea or not. I mean, it does cost a lot of money to be a missionary. You have to pay for your own medical insurance, retirement, travel, housing, and everything else, and you are completely out there on your own. If you're going to survive, you gotta raise the dough. But in America, running around and broadcasting your personal finances isn't exactly normal procedure. I was in a quandary.

I ran it by Brad. He gave me some good strategies, but ultimately said, honesty is the best way. I went back to the businessman with the rundown and disclosed our financial reality to anybody else who asked. Everybody seemed satisfied; honesty worked.

Then, once we got to Kenya, I was really weirded out by the fact that most missionaries have nationals helping them in and around their homes. It felt really strange being an employer and paying such low wages, despite the fact that these people were desperate for work and money. However, the relationships we formed with these workers were very much like family, and it seemed really sneaky to try and hide the importance of these people in our lives.

I emailed Brad. As a former missionary of twenty years, he understood the dilemma. He suggested that I carefully but honestly explain the working relationships to my family and supporters in the U.S. We didn't receive any negative feedback from sharing the information, and again, honesty prevailed.

Other situations have come up—whether theological or relational or financial—and Brad is always good for an honest answer. And the advice that mostly comes back has one theme—be honest.

This advice sits pretty well with me. I tend to be a very honest person on the page and a fairly honest person face-to-face. I feel like honesty is important for missionaries for a few reasons.

First off—missionaries often get put on a pedestal, at home and abroad. When I'm honest about how I hid inside my house with the lights off to avoid a visitor, and how I raced a guy for ten miles who cut me off on the highway, that makes me seem more real to non-missionaries. I'm a fallen creature just like everyone else. No pedestals here.

Secondly, I think that honesty is the best way to show the active ways that God is redeeming me. I don't want to be selfish with my private time or succumb to road rage, so I need God's help to be a better me. If I portray only my good side to those around me on the mission field, then I'm kind of lying. Maybe not outright, but I'm lying by omission. Even those I'm seeking to convert need to see the "real" me and not some squeaky clean phony.

Another thing that honesty does is bring missions home for supporters. By allowing my supporters to connect with me on a real level, they will know me—my strengths and my weaknesses—a whole lot better. Through that connection, we will work together better at the task at hand. Also, it brings missions home by showing that I and the issues I face there are similar in many ways to the people at home and their issues. Missions and missionaries aren't as foreign when they see the common ground between us.

If you've read up until this point, you've probably heard an embarrassing story or two. You've probably been a little shocked by something about my life in Africa. There's a good chance that I've offended you with something I've thought or confessed.

But I have to ask—is that bad? Are you surrounded in your day-to-day life with people who don't shock or disappoint you or anger you at times? Probably not. When it comes to real life, the way you and I actually live may not be the way we *think* we should be living or the way that books tell us we should be living. Life is a tad messy for all of us, missionary or not.

Paul says he wants to happily boast of his weaknesses, so that God's grace will come through even more powerfully. While many of us will brag about God's grace in our lives—as well we should!—few of us like to look dumb or weak or broken or insufficient. Those don't seem like comely poses for a respectable Christian to assume. And when it comes to leaders of the faith—like pastors or elders or missionaries—heaven forbid we be anything but perfect.

Yet power is made perfect in weakness.

We will do well to remember that as missionaries. Our personal weaknesses can be the vehicles for God's grace to come into our ministries. We don't need to dwell unhealthily on our sin; that can lead to a twisted focus on self rather than God when it comes to the message of our lives. But to hide our sin and present a perfect exterior is actually the furthest thing we can do from striving for perfection. God's perfect power only manifests itself when we tell the truth, when we're 100% transparent about what we can and cannot do.

There's a good chance we'll do something stupid as missionaries, with or without help from friends like Brad, but that doesn't doom us to failure. In fact, it may open up a window for God.

Stories of Living

The discovery of "blogging" was a joyful event for me. Sharing both the funny and difficult things in life was essential as I transitioned into the missionary life. Prayer letter and email updates are great, but I tend to keep them a little more serious and to-the-point. My blog—*Strangers in Kenya*—is where I can be me. This chapter's stories are a random collection of honest snippets from my blog.

A game well played

At our staff meeting on Wednesday, a man stood up who graduated from Rift Valley Academy in 1958 and worked on staff here for many years. After thanking us for our prayers on behalf of his family, he asked, "Who is the Penn State fan here?" I raised my fist in the air, which prompted him to chant, "We are..." I knew the appropriate response—"Penn State!" He had seen the tire cover on the back of my SUV and knew there was another Lion fan roaming the campus these days.

The reason he had come back to visit us was to bury and to celebrate the memory of his identical twin brother John. John and his wife Elaine live here on campus, and John served the school (in recent years) by being our visa/immigration/tax guy to the Kenyan government, no small feat for a faculty of around 70. During his forty years of service at RVA (yes, 40!), he had done just about every other job imaginable—teaching, dorm parenting, administration. His wife has built a growing ministry to orphans in recent years (called "Little Lambs") and will continue in her work even now that he's gone.

In a beautiful display of love, over 300 students attended a memorial service yesterday, despite the fact that few of them knew him well. To see young people—the same ones who will be world-changers and missionaries in the future—honoring the past legacy of a man who devoted his life of 68 years to the Lord's work on this continent was a beautiful tribute.

The verse that the Lord brought to mind this week was 1 Peter 2:5: "You also, like living stones, are being built into a spiritual house to be a holy priesthood, offering spiritual sacrifices acceptable to God through Jesus Christ."

John is no longer a "living stone" here among us, but his time on earth has left a firm foundation. And the "spiritual house" that is RVA will forever be more stable and strong because of him.

You can pray for this family (his two children are now missionaries themselves working in South Africa and Tanzania) as they go through this time of mourning and transition. I'll take care of his brother tonight. We're planning to listen to the Penn St.-Purdue football game on Internet radio together at my house. Of course we're hoping for a PSU win, but I'm also hoping to learn through his brother more about this great man who went on to glory this week.

Killer threes

This past weekend there were three "killer threes" in my life. Two of them were killers in the bad sense, and one of them was a killer in the good sense. Like the way Keanu Reeves said "killer dude!" in the surf movie *Point Break*.

I'll list them in order.

My JV girls basketball season is winding down. We've had a great season—10 wins, 1 loss, and first place in our league of Nairobi area schools. For an extra challenge, we played in a varsity tournament on Saturday. In the knockout round of the tournament, we faced our school's own varsity team. The game went as expected, and we were trailing by 7 points (in a shortened game due to tournament rules) with two minutes to go. I was about to empty my bench when our press defense heated up. I kept the starters in, and then with 25 seconds left, we trailed by just two. Our point guard shot a beautiful three (she hadn't made one all season) that found nothing but net. The crowd of about 200 RVA fans went ballistic for the JV underdog.

Stacy, our varsity coach, called timeout after a near turnover. The clock read :10. I had two things in my head to tell my girls defensively. One—shift down to the baseline if they try to attack us from the wing. And two—*what was two?* I forgot. I told them I couldn't remember and to go have fun—JV teams aren't supposed to beat varsity teams!

As varsity in-bounded the ball, I suddenly remembered what I wanted to tell them. "Don't let #6 shoot an outside shot!" The ball went to #6, #6 launched a perfect three pointer, and the ball again found nothing but net. The crowd went wild again (it's hard to go wrong as fans when both of your teams are playing), and we couldn't get a shot off in the final five seconds.

It was a good loss, to say the least. My team had nothing to be ashamed of, and there were lots of hugs between both teams from RVA after the game.

The next killer three came from a sporting event I wasn't present for in body although in my heart I was. If you are a long-time reader of my blog, you've probably noticed the sidebar link that says "2009 National Champions." Well, truth is, I've been updating that link every year since 2005—waiting, hoping, praying that my Penn State football team would one day fulfill my prophecy. It hasn't happened yet. But this year, this year, it was primed to happen. We won the game against Purdue that I listened to with John's brother, we beat our toughest foe on the road (Ohio State), and we were one of the few undefeated teams left in the country. Our last three games were against lesser foes, and a trip to the national championship game seemed very, very possible.

But it wasn't to be. Another killer three came along.

Listening to the game on Internet radio (very choppy feed but I heard enough to follow along), I was barely awake at 2:30 a.m. on Sunday morning. Penn State had dominated the whole game, but the scoreboard didn't show it. Iowa drove down the field with just minutes left and set up for a field goal. With six seconds left on the clock, the kick went up for Iowa and down came Penn State's hopes for an undefeated season. The three points put Iowa ahead 24-23, and Penn State had no chance for a comeback.

And so next year, I'll change the sidebar to "2010 National Champions" and keep waiting, hoping, praying it comes true.

All right. On to the good "killer" three. (My San Diego friends know how to say it with the proper inflection.) Dozens of friends and supporters were part of our huge fundraiser to buy a car in 2006. We certainly stretched the uppermost limits of our budget to get an amazingly sound vehicle, but, in the process, we missed out on some of the crucial "extras" needed for Kenyan roads—like metal grills to cover the lights, a roof rack, and extra seats.

One of the extras I wrote about last spring in my "Lesson for Lasting" about humor—two extra seats for the back of our LandCruiser. The second "extra" we've been able to add to our vehicle just came along last month—a roof rack.

Two months ago, I spotted an SUV like ours with the perfect design for a roof rack. I asked the owner where he had it made and how much. It was from a quality company and cost him $900. Well, *that* wasn't going to happen. Not at that price. But I have a Kenyan friend who is a welder, and we drew up some designs (modeled after the one I saw). He made it for me in one week, and the total cost of the thing was under $140.

We took it on its maiden voyage on Sunday—the four Murphys inside and three single RVA missionaries. With four family units looking to buy enough groceries for three weeks, you can see why we needed the roof rack. We filled three containers on the roof (at least 60 pounds each) and still needed to fill in all of the cracks inside the car with stuff. But the trip was successful, and the roof rack was just one more blessing to us that we've been able to use to bless others—*three* others this time! A killer three, dude.

Thanksgiving thought

This is what I felt like Wednesday: Woke up at 6. Taught classes until 10. Graded papers until noon. Drove through Nairobi city traffic until 6 p.m. while taking students to the airport. Finalized my grades until 9. Sat down for a prayer meeting until 10.

This is what I felt like Thursday: All 400-plus students are gone. Grades are in. My wife was filling our house with wonderful smells. My boys were laughing and fighting and playing. Eight guests came over for the late lunch turkey celebration. We then ate a variety of pies for dinner. And snacked on leftover sandwiches at 9 p.m.

Russian novelist Fyodor Dostoevsky said, "The best definition of man is a being that goes on two legs and is ungrateful." That's probably why our ancestors saw fit to create a holiday to overcome the worst tendency in us—ingratitude. A lot to be thankful for here. I hope you are thankful too.

WINTER

Lessons for Lasting *Worship*

Exodus 8:1b
"This is what the Lord says: Let my people go, so that they may worship me."

I've been a little overwhelmed with life lately. On top of the normal frenetic pace of school, my wife's schedule has been insane. As an organizer for the AIM women's retreat, she has been feverishly working up until this past weekend for the retreat. Also, she's a class sponsor in charge of coordinating a drama/musical for our school's version of prom. In the midst of her busyness, my busyness also has increased as I help out more around the house. Sadly, when I get busy, it's often my time alone with God that suffers.

So this morning, while I was watching the boys, I knew I wouldn't be able to lock myself in my room and spend some time with the Lord. I knew that a traditional "quiet time" wouldn't happen. But I needed so desperately to be close to Him and have Him breathe new life in my dry soul. I had to do something.

I opened a 15-pound bag of dry powdered cheese sauce.

First off, the cheese sauce was sent by my elementary physical education teacher (that's a story all in itself) who knows about my sons' addictions to macaroni and cheese. He found some bulk bags of it and sent it our way. While my boys do really love mac-n-cheese, they can't eat a vat full of it in one sitting. When I broke open this box this morning, I set myself to the task of breaking the seven huge bags down into 100 small bags.

And that's where I found myself back at the foot of the cross. As my fingers repetitively scooped and dumped and cinched, scooped and dumped and cinched, I found my mind focusing on God's welcoming embrace. As the cheese powder fumes caked the inside of my nose and mouth, I found myself breathing out prayers that I hadn't been real enough to express in weeks.

The boys left me alone. After all, I was just busy doing work in the kitchen in their eyes. I had one hour with God, a better hour than I've had in weeks, all by myself, in the kitchen, standing over a bowl of artificial cheese powder.

We should never stop worshiping, and the ironic thing is that I do sometimes. Here I am, someone whose life purpose is to see God worshiped among the nations, and yet I fail to worship God at times. It's baffling.

The oft half-quoted verse from Exodus 8 gives us a good reminder of God's intention for us. Here was a group of people that had a lot of problems—social outcasts in a foreign land, physically and emotionally beaten down as slaves, spiritually restricted by the land's rulers—and they knew it. Their pain led them to cry out to God, and He heard them. But when Moses delivered God's command to Pharoah, he revealed that God's number one priority for the enslaved Hebrews had nothing to do with them at all.

He didn't say, "Let my people go because they are socially awkward or because they are physically exhausted or emotionally depressed or spiritually empty." He said, "Let my people go, so that they may worship me."

Worship was missing.

It's ironic that Moses' words often get cut off at "Let my people go" today because it reflects our true priorities when relating to God. We like that God likes us. We like that he wants us to be free. We like it when we're socially, physically, emotionally, and spiritually healthy. But we totally miss the point of all these things. Anything that we have going for us in life is solely for the sake of worship. The last part of this verse is far more important in God's eyes—"so that they may worship me."

Without the worship of God in this scenario, the Hebrew nation might as well have shriveled up and died in slavery. Countless other cultures have gone this way throughout history. Overthrown, then oppressed, and finally extinct. The Hebrews could have been just another lost culture. But there was more to their story. They were God's people, and the only fitting response to the one true God is worship.

As missionaries, we can get so busy with building our houses and starting new relationships that we forget why we're there. We can spend every waking minute learning language and teaching the Bible that we lose sight of the reasons we do it.

Our very presence in a foreign culture can become sadly ironic. Our lives can begin to shout out the phrase, "Let my people go," while we forget why we want them to be free in the first place.

"So that they may worship me" is the real reason we're here. But how will they ever learn to worship if we ourselves have forgotten?

May we make every effort to worship him every day, but if we lose our way, I pray that God will show up and help us, whether it be through a tongue-tied bearded guy with a staff or through artificial cheese flavoring.

Stories of Living

Opportunities to worship lurk in every corner. The first story "Let it no! Let it no! Let it no!" tells of worship during the Christmas season, whether living in plenty or in want. "Missionary romance" explains how two hearts becoming one gives us reason to praise God. "An American band in Kenya?" describes a rare chance I had to worship God through familiar music despite being in Africa. Finally, "Senseless death" explores the pain of poverty that forces us to find worship in tragedy.

Let it no! Let it no! Let it no!

Merry Christmas! As I write this, the family (plus adopted Auntie Jess who is a dorm mom at Rift Valley Academy this year) sits in the living room playing with Christmas presents. We had an amazing morning full of new treasures, thanks mostly to our friends and family in the U.S. who sent us a bounty of gifts.

While most of the U.S. seems to be experiencing snow already this season, we here in Kenya are not. In fact, it's the opposite. It's summer in the Southern Hemisphere and so it's been in the 80's, dry, and sunny nearly every day of the last two months. While you all are singing, "Let it snow!" this Christmas, our world seems to be echoing "Let it no!"

No rain. Yesterday afternoon, after the missionary community had delivered over 60 food baskets to widows in the community, it seemed like our prayers would be answered. Dark clouds and rolling thunder swept across the hillside and filled the vast valley. We thought maybe, just maybe, God would give us a little extra Christmas present in the form of rain. Alas, it wasn't to be. Perhaps another community miles away received the rain but not ours. A weak season of crops is going to compound the problems of an already struggling economy in this country.

The word "no." Asher is learning to talk, and his favorite word right now is "no." No matter what we ask him to do, he barks out "No!" Even if we're offering candy or toys, he'll still feel obligated to say "No!" before he eagerly takes the attractive item. He's learning other words now too, though. He learned how to say, "Ho, ho, ho! Merry Christmas!" from a *Bob the Builder* DVD Heather's mom sent. It sounds more like "Ho, ho, ho! Merry Meez" but we've enjoyed every one of the thousand times he's said it this week, nevertheless.

No water. This time it's not "rain related." A pipe in our neighbor's yard started leaking yesterday (Christmas Eve morning) and by the time we were ready to go caroling at the children's ward of the local hospital, it was a fountain. They had to shut off the pipe (which supplies eight houses in our part of campus with water), and the work crew won't come back to work until Monday; Kenyans don't "do" emergencies on their days off. My missionary neighbor Michael (who still has water) filled up a drum for us, and this will be our little well until early next week.

No family. This is actually only our second "family-less" Christmas since we've been on the mission field; 2005 was our other. Heather's parents were here in 2006, and we were in the U.S. for December 2007. Those past memories are sweet though, and the anticipation of our home assignment next year definitely is making this Christmas less lonely.

No regrets. We're lucky to be part of God's work in Africa. No sacrifice we make could make us regret that we're here. He's given us more than we could deserve.

Missionary romance

All right. It's Valentines Day, and I'm a sucker for a good love story.

There are a handful of single people who joined the RVA team this past fall, some short-termers and some long-termers. These singles have meshed right into the fabric of things here, and they really seem to enjoy one another's company as well.

One of the long-termers is an elementary school teacher named Erica. As the fall wore on, it turned out that she was enjoying the company of a certain short-term missionary named Matt. Now, Matt was a dentist down at the hospital, and although he wasn't school staff, he was still involved with the school and had lots of friendships up here.

Although our missionary community here is quite a fish bowl at times, we try to respect each other's privacy and whatnot. While everyone noticed the time Matt and Erica were spending together, no one pried to see if it was "more" than just friendship. Matt's short-term assignment ended, and he went back to the United States at Christmas.

Matt and Erica continued to write emails, and (as we found out this week) they were in fact dating long distance. (Does it get any more long distance for humankind to be romantically involved from Africa to North America?) They were writing and calling and things were going along swimmingly.

Well, last week, Matt had supposedly sent a package to Erica from America that his friends here in Kijabe were going to deliver for him. These friends borrowed Erica's house keys while she was at work under the ruse of "delivering the package" for her. What they did was fill the house with hundreds of roses and put a chair in front of the TV. They returned her keys to her and told her that she had to go directly into her apartment alone, sit down, and watch a video. She did. It was Matt on the screen holding up cue cards with the song's romantic lyrics on them. And when the romantic song ended (the last cue cards read "I love you"), Matt began reading from 1 Corinthians 13 from the kitchen behind her.

Not on video, but in person! He had come back to Africa without telling her. She had no idea he was on the continent, let alone in her apartment. And that wasn't all. After he finished reading, he got down on one knee and asked her to be his wife.

He had letters of congratulations from his parents and her parents ahead of time (they all knew about his trip and his plan, but kept it from her) and when he got up off his knee, he had her answer.

Yes!

An American band in Kenya?

Saturday night I got a phone call with some crazy news. Jars of Clay would be performing in Nairobi on Sunday. After some juggling of schedules and responsibilities, I took a carload of RVA staff into the city for the concert. It was my first rock concert in over four years (our entire time in Kenya), so you can imagine my excitement.

The concert promoted the Jijue 1 Million Campaign. The message of the campaign—to encourage 1 million Kenyans to get tested for HIV by the end of 2010—was sprinkled in by artists and by local radio DJs. Jars of Clay was able to headline the show due to their travel with Blood:Water Mission (an organization they founded).

Dozens of warm-up acts—yes, dozens—crammed the stage for the first two and a half hours, and then around 4:30, we finally saw *wazungu* (white people) start to assemble on the stage. Our attention perked up from the back of the room; my friend Ryan even picked out a few band members on stage doing their own set-up. I'm sure that's not the protocol they're used to on American tours, but here in Africa, the band seemed to roll with things pretty well. The emcees of the event decided that they had been stalling for time long enough and that Jars of Clay should have been ready. They did their big "Ladies and gentlemen, Jars of Clay!" announcement and walked off stage to thunderous applause. Hilariously, the band and the stagehands continued their preparations for another five minutes. When the band finally was ready, they simply walked to the mics and began their set themselves.

The show kicked off with their legendary anthem "Flood," which still receives a lot of radio play here in Kenya today. Lead singer Dan Haseltine told the crowd that they'd chosen some "oldies" for the Nairobi crowd, perhaps because it's easier for people here to get older, used music than it is to get newer releases. Besides "Flood" there was "Liquid," "Love song for a Savior," and "Crazy times," and the audience loved singing along with all of the classics.

Perhaps the most difficult part of the concert for me was Heseltine's "apology" to Africans on behalf of America as he introduced "Light gives heat." In a message of empowerment, he apologized to the Kenyan crowd for Western influence on their country, saying that they shouldn't be told how to "raise their children and fix their communities" by the "heroes from the West," echoing lines from the song. As a missionary giving my life to help (not to belittle or to perpetuate dependency among Africans), I felt a little awkward standing among the 95% Kenyan crowd. I know the band is doing missions work themselves; their Blood:Water Mission is an American enterprise championing the cause of poor Africans. So, I really don't think his aim was at bashing people like me, but I still didn't quite know how to feel as one who supposedly needed to "apologize" for being in Africa.

The band wrapped up the day with "Carry Me (Dead Man)" and "Revolution," and the crowd would have easily rocked along for two more hours if they could have. There were little kids way in the back dancing freestyle and adults in the front breakdancing. Things really did seem to be picking up just when it was time to wind down.

As we walked out of the building, one of the girls in our group dragged us back inside. She made a contact with the concert organizer, and she said the band wanted to meet us. We waited about 10 minutes and then one by one, the band emerged from the green room. Dan told us about his encounter with Kenyan customs (they barely released their instruments in time for their first show), Charlie (keyboard) knew about our school because his wife was a missionary kid herself, and a few people got their pictures taken with the guys. Like most Christian performers I've met through the years, the guys were completely humble and fun to chat with. I thanked them all profusely for not just investing their time and money in declaring God's glory to Africa, but also for giving us a chance to worship God with familiar music, instruments, and accents in a foreign land.

Senseless death

We have a baby-sized Wal-Mart here in Kenya. It's called Nakumatt and is operated by a South African conglomerate. We hit Nakumatt about once a month and stock up big time. But last week's sad headline about Nakumatt proves that while Western methods of shopping may have arrived in Africa, traditional sensibilities and fears still reign.

At least 49 people died in a Nakumatt fire last week. As smoke started filling the large store, the generator went off and left hundreds of customers in darkness. As they fought their way through the dark store towards the lit exits, they found the doors locked.

Locked exits in a fire? Are you serious?

The employees were so in fear of immediate looting (a real fear) that they locked the doors to keep potential looters inside the store in and looters who might come from the outside out. What they did instead, tragically, was lock dozens of people inside a burning building.

Poverty and theft are so rampant in Africa that the employees of a successful business allowed their petty responsibilities overstep their human responsibilities to protect and save their fellow man. Forty-nine lives lost in order to potentially save a few thousand dollars worth of merchandise. Such a sad clashing of worlds.

And then on Saturday, another money-related disaster in Molo, Kenya. A fuel tanker overturned on a busy roadway. Instead of staying clear of the dangerous situation, poor Kenyans ran to the spill with containers. They wanted to take advantage of the free fuel. The hapless truck driver attempted to salvage something good from his mistake so he began charging people to steal fuel from his wrecked vehicle. Allegedly, an angry man who had no money to pay the truck driver decided to lash out.

He lit the accident site on fire.

Over 100 are confirmed dead. Dozens more are suffering from severe burns and more are likely to die from their wounds.

Truck wrecks can happen anywhere. Store fires can happen anywhere. It's not like those two incidents were the tragedies. The tragic thing is when the basic need for survival overshadows basic laws of safety and multiplies the disastrous effects of disasters.

It'll be interesting to see what fall-out results from these two preposterous tragedies. Government regulations? Employee training programs? Different policies on security when disasters occur? More common sense teaching of the dangers of fuel and fire?

Or will Kenyans lash out at some secondary target like Nakumatt or a trucking company, rather than acknowledge that their real enemy is abject poverty and the stupid things it makes people do?

SPRING

Lessons for Lasting
Fellowship

Hebrews 10:24-25
"And let us consider how we may spur one another on toward love and good deeds. Let us not give up meeting together, as some are in the habit of doing, but let us encourage one another—and all the more as you see the Day approaching."

Perhaps the biggest shock of the missions life for me has been in the area of relationships. I had expectations of a *Band of Brothers*-like experience. After all, we'd be working along side men and women with similar passions and talents, working towards the same goals, and we'd be relying on and needing each other for everything. I'd heard from other missionaries that "you'll make the closest relationships you'll ever make on the mission field."

I know, I know. Pretty lofty expectations. And those expectations have made the reality of life here even more difficult.

The reality is there are about a hundred great men and women here who pour themselves into their various ministries. And when they get time off, they enjoy time with their families or with visitors from North America. Finally, when the pie chart of time is divvied out, the one area that seems to be absent or miniscule is that of adult relationships. It also seems like the time spent on peer interactions among missionaries gets shared among so many great people (one week we'll visit with Family X and the next with Family Y) that it's hard to form deeper bonds with any particular person or people. At least, this has been my experience.

The one saving grace, for me, has been the length of my stay in Africa. A lot of people are here for a month or two, or maybe even a year or two, and then are gone. With the limited amount of time to forge relationships in general, trying to create something meaningful and lasting with these people is a frustrating endeavor. However, since my wife and I are "career" missionaries, we've had almost four years now to get to know other career missionaries.

The benefits of longer relationships are obvious. But in this context, there is one deeper blessing.

Transitions and loss are a constant way of life here. People are coming and going almost on a daily basis, and when you compound that steady emotional turmoil with the pressures of living in a cross-cultural setting, the burden is huge. Luckily, we have some brothers and sisters here who are planning and hoping on being here for decades, and without those friends— even though we're not extremely close—I'm not sure how I'd hold up.

In light of this, this spring season has been a doozy. We're preparing for our first home assignment beginning in July. After four years of service on the field, our agency allows for one year of furlough to reconnect with supporters and raise additional finances. Already facing the prospect of saying goodbye to our school's junior and senior class for good (the seniors will be leaving for college when we leave this summer and the juniors will graduate during our year of home assignment), we got news that some good friends with four little kids around our kids' ages wouldn't be coming back due to lack of financial support. They had already been here a decade and hoped to be here for life.

Then, last week, the staff received a long, shocking email describing how Wally, the student chaplain, and his nurse wife were being led by the Lord (against their human will) to return to the U.S.[1]

We've gotten used to saying hello and goodbye to people here on a frequent basis—but when "career" people are taken out from under us, it's especially hard to take. Losing Wally, though, is one of the hardest losses of all. You may be thinking—*hold on, you're getting ready for home assignment...you yourself are leaving that place...how can you be lamenting other people leaving RVA?* That's a great point, but as we leave, it's comforting to know what and who will still be here when we come back. These career people are the backbone of our school, and losing a key piece of your vertebrae (like Wally and his wife Donna) can turn your heart into a joyless jellyfish.

Wally has been one of my closest friends in a place where I've lacked close friends. He's been a coaching mentor for basketball (he's the varsity coach) and a fellow fan of college football (even though he's allied with the dark force of unholy wickedness, i.e. Ohio State). He's taught me a lot about student ministry and activities, and he's a great preacher as well. It's said that every Christian should have a Timothy (referring to how Paul mentored the younger Timothy in the Bible) and a Barnabas in his life (referring to Paul's friendship with his peer), and I really felt like I was a Timothy to Wally. He is/was a great mentor for me, and knowing that he will be leaving RVA was a hard blow to me.

My tearful prayers on the night I found out consisted mainly of questions. *How can you take him? Why now? Who will fill his void, both in my life and for the school? Why?*

---

[1] I know what kind of man pops into your head when you hear the name "Wally"—dorky, skinny, glasses, toilet paper stuck to his shoe—but you'll have to let go of that. He's a 50-year-old jock with a Marine haircut who dresses like a Foot Locker mannequin, the most un-Wally-like Wally you'll ever meet.

Not all prayers are answered. This is a simple fact of faith. And technically, my prayers from the night before weren't answered the next misty morning as I went for a walk and listened to a sermon on my iPod. What I got, however, was better than an answer. I got a reason.

God walked beside me down that muddy African road, listening to Francis Chan from California preach on Colossians 1:24.

"Now I rejoice in what was suffered for you, and I fill up in my flesh what is still lacking in regard to Christ's affliction, for the sake of his body, which is the church."

First off, this verse does not imply that Christ's sacrifice on the cross is lacking. His payment for sin is perfect, once and for all, and sufficient to redeem all mankind.

So what is "lacking" then? Francis gave a few interpretations, but the one that made most sense to me was this.

We are Christ's body in this world. He has no feet and hands in this world or any kind of physical manifestation except through us. We who believe in him are his church, the "body" of Christ. If we are like him, we should resemble him in every way. In the way he lived, loved, healed, gave, and sacrificed. Our words shouldn't just speak of sacrificial love; our lives should exhibit it.

Jesus Christ was able to persevere through the shame and pain of the cross in Jerusalem in 30 A.D., but he has never had a chance to persevere in the face of suffering at Rift Valley Academy in 2009. My puny story "fills up what is still lacking in regard to Christ's affliction" because I can show the world what it means to love God right here, right now. This pain I'm feeling over losing friends—and particularly Wally—is a glorious opportunity for me to "rejoice" for the sake of the church.

God hasn't sent us suffering for the sake of suffering. God's car doesn't have the bumper sticker "No Pain, No Gain" on the back of it. Suffering is part of life on earth, but to God, it's our opportunity to offer our measly sacrifice alongside of

Christ's enormous sacrifice and boldly announce—"I'm with him! I want to be like him! Look at me if you want to see a tiny glimpse of him, right here, right now."

In areas of fellowship, missionaries frequently find suffering. Whether you are the only missionary within a thousand miles or surrounded by a giant team of them, fellowship is hard to come by. Sometimes you'll find friends, but they won't share your faith. Sometimes you'll find brothers and sisters in Christ who you don't necessarily get along with. Whatever your particular scenario, fellowship must be sought and even fought for on the mission field.

The writer of Hebrews 10:24-25 emphasizes that the reason for fellowship is to spur one another to good works. But I think he skips the result of fellowship—full hearts. I think that good fellowship fills up our love tank. From that abundance, we can overflow into the lives of others through our ministry. If that tank is low, we can still go on. But not for long. I've known a few missionaries who hated their time at our school—a school filled with other Western believers and seemingly bursting with fellowship opportunities—because they didn't find encouragement or fellowship within our gates. When tanks are empty, people bolt.

For those of us who refuse to balk in our calling to missions, the lessons are simple. Number one—we must fight to find fellowship. And number two—we must offer the fellowship we are lacking as a beautiful sacrifice to God.

Stories of Living

After four years in Africa, this season would be our last, for a while. Home assignment is a part of every missionary's life, and we were looking forward to a year stateside to catch up with family, reconnect with supporters, and build up our support team for our next stint in Africa. The stories in this section focus on the strange feelings of gearing up for a new phase of life while winding down a familiar one overseas.

Mercy and grace

One of my favorite (but most time-consuming) tasks as an English teacher is reading journals. I start my students off on a topic, but then allow them to branch off if need be. While reading journals this past term (we're on Easter break right now so the students are at their homes in various countries in Africa), a slight, smiley blond girl named Ruthie inspired me the most.

She shared one story of how she and her Kenyan friends were out playing in the village during her childhood. Her fair, fair skin and blond hair set her apart from the other children in everyone's mind but hers. So, when a white person drove through their village, she joined in with the children in their ritual. *Mzungu* means white person in Swahili, and for some reason, Kenyans feel compelled (adult Kenyans too!) to vocalize the fact that white people are white. It's part-taunt, part-exclamation. Little Ruthie ran after the car, yelling "Mzungu, mzungu," oblivious to the fact that she herself was a mzungu. It turned out that the white person in the car was actually visiting her family, and the driver didn't appreciate the heckling that her hosts' little white daughter participated in.

But it was another story which Ruthie shared that I'd like to pass along as an Easter meditation.

Her parents came to Africa to start a children's home, an orphanage for abandoned street children. Due to the AIDS pandemic, the larger towns and cities of Africa are flooded with such children. While they built their living quarters and the orphanage, they lived out of their car and began to befriend the children of their village. One day, a boy stole Ruthie's mother's purse, an inconvenient setback and discouragement.

Months later, when the buildings were complete, Ruthie's mom went back out on the streets to find the thief. When she found him, she told him that she wanted to help him change his life and invited him to come live in the home with them. He accepted the offer, accepted the unconditional love and forgiveness from Ruthie's family, and eventually accepted

Christ as his savior. Now, he has a job and is a young man living for God.

Ruthie wrote this journal entry in response to the topic, "What are mercy and grace?"

Mercy is not getting what we deserve. This boy deserved punishment for his crime, and the prison systems here are vicious, brutal places. This boy deserved anger and hatred from Ruthie's mom for the sin he committed against her. This boy did not get what he deserved. He got mercy.

Grace is getting what we don't deserve. Some would say that this boy didn't deserve the opportunity Ruthie's family gave him. Some would say that missions work is too expensive and too hard on the missionary families and too ineffective to really change the world. But then you take a look at grace in action—salvation, redemption, renewal—and it's hard to allow ungraciousness to live on inside your heart.

Because in your heart—if you believe in Easter—you find mercy and grace, not coming from inside you but coming from outside you. The mercy of the Father…not punishing you for your sins. The grace of Christ…giving you joy here and paradise eternally.

And if it's inside of you, how can you not let it out? How can you not share it with your family members and co-workers—so hurting from the toils of life and weight of their sins? How can you not strive for a way to get it to every corner of the earth, to the places where "mercy" and "grace" are alien concepts?

Ruthie's story didn't end there. Once this street boy, this orphan thief, found work, he bought a present for the family who did so much for him. He bought Ruthie's mother a purse and filled it. He thought back to the day of the crime, and he tried to remember everything that he had taken from her, the things he sold for money. He filled the new purse in remembrance of mercy; he filled the new purse with small tokens of new grace. He returned Ruthie's mom's display of mercy and grace in the symbolism of a new purse.

And he did all this because Jesus rose from the grave, because mercy and grace are alive.

Threadbare

Threadbare: adj. 1. worn down so that the threads show 2. wearing old, worn clothes; shabby 3. that has lost its freshness or novelty

This expressive vocabulary word has long been one of my favorites. It's such a visual word that I've commonly used it to describe my patience with someone, or perhaps the supply of food in our cabinets, or maybe my enjoyment or interest in something.

The irony is that lately I've found myself thinking about this word every morning while dressing. It turns out that this word's literal meaning actually still applies in certain situations. Like with my socks. And my pants. And my shirts. And my shoes. And my, um, undergarments.

Nearly four years ago, we were in the U.S. stocking up on clothing to last us for four years, and now that the four years are almost up, guess what? The clothing has lasted, but is now threadbare.

My thick black socks still have areas of thickness, but for the most part, they are threadbare. While few of my pants have actual holes, the cuffs of each are beyond threadbare; they are stringy and frayed. My first set of shoes are long gone, by the way, and my second stringers—found used at local markets in Kenya—are developing holes and losing their soles (a truly perilous thing for a missionary). And I'm pretty sure these t-shirts and underwear weren't see-through when I bought them.

Coming from a middle class, Western background, it's uncomfortable for me to get "dressed up" for teaching every morning with less-than-best dress clothes. But at this point—less than three months until we're back in the U.S.—it's silly to think of shopping for anything less holey and more thread-ful than what I currently have. And as these final weeks of our first term of service wear on in Kenya (no pun intended), I think my definition of "threadbare" will become even more transparently clear (still no pun intended).

Lions

The highlight of Kenya's tourism is the wildlife. Going on an African safari doesn't get much better than it does in Kenya. And the keystone of all African animals is none other than the king of the jungle—the lion.

We've found ourselves on a few safaris—sometimes in tour vans and sometimes in our own vehicle—and searching for lions is certainly a highlight. Leopards and cheetahs are more rare to find, but nothing is more majestic than a lion.

One time, we were driving through a wooded area, and we found another vehicle just pulling away from looking at something. We stopped. About 30 feet away was a half-eaten zebra being gnawed on by a lion. We pulled our truck as close to the kill site as we could and went crazy with our cameras. Then, the lion disappeared. We backed the truck up, trying for a different angle in the dense forest. We could still see the red, black, and white zebra, but the lion was out of view. For a while.

Suddenly, we spotted the lion walking parallel to the road about twenty feet away from us. I now was less concerned about pictures and became more concerned with getting my 3-year-old (at the time) son away from the window and getting the car into drive in case I needed to bolt.

The feeling changed from "hunter" to "hunted" in a few seconds. The elation we felt over seeing a lion in the wild—and seeing a lion in the middle of a meal, no less—morphed into terror as this lion appeared within striking distance.

I tell this story as an analogy. We've been looking forward to going back to the U.S. for months now, if not years. The family, the friends, the food, the familiarity—all have been calling to us from this unusual land of our mission sojourn. The years became seasons, the seasons became months, the months became weeks, and now the weeks are just days. Sixteen to be exact. The excitement and the suspense of "going home" are turning—like our emotions on safari when the beast appeared just yards from us—into something much more complicated. We're packing up our house in Africa. We'll be living out of suitcases for 12 months in America. We're leaving our full-time ministry and careers in Africa. We'll be doing a lot of different things—very little teaching—for the next year in America. We'll be leaving our relationships (hundreds of students and dozens of missionary staff and Kenyan nationals) in Africa. We'll be renewing hundreds of old relationships and starting dozens of new ones in America. Suddenly, Africa has become more familiar to us than America, and going "home" feels different.

I know there is no reason for fear. God has promised never to leave us or forsake us, just as he promised Joshua in Deuteronomy 31:6. He sustained us when we moved to Kenya in 2005, carrying us through those tough transitions. He'll sustain us this month as we move and adjust back to our "old life" in America.

But that truth doesn't minimize the fact that right now I'm staring into the eyes of the lion and feeling like I want to put my foot on the gas.

Patty Hearst and me

For my older readers, no explanation of this title is probably necessary. For those of you who are younger, you might need a quick pop history lesson.

In 1974, Patty Hearst—the 19-year-old millionaire daughter of publishing's legendary Hearst family—was kidnapped by the Symbionese Liberation Army in Berkeley, CA. Two months later, bank video cameras caught her brandishing a machine gun during a bank robbery with the SLA. When she was finally arrested along with her kidnappers, she called herself an "urban guerilla" and was committed to the causes of the SLA. Her family's ritzy attorneys couldn't convince a jury that she wasn't a willing participant in the crimes; she got 35 years in prison (later shortened by Jimmy Carter).

Today, Hearst symbolizes the desire to break away from normal society and live anarchically. She also stands as a prototypical case of the "Stockholm Syndrome," a phenomenon where captives begin to care for and empathize with their captors. Rather than hating and distancing themselves from their jailors, prisoners will begin to love their familiar surroundings.

As my time in Africa winds down, I find myself thinking about this crazy story from 1974. For much of my four years here, I adamantly preferred my old way of life in America. The easy life. Friends and family close by. Abundant free time. Familiar cultural surroundings. Fast food—tasty, cheap, and easy to come by. I gladly settled in here, knowing that my work for God's kingdom was far more important than a lifestyle preference, but nevertheless, if I had to choose…

But I'm starting to feel like Patty Hearst. I actually think I'm going to miss the bumpy roads and the daily electricity outages. I can see myself longing for all of my wife's yummy meals from scratch when pre-made frozen meals and fast food become regular again. The spiders, the dust, the monkeys wailing, the roosters crowing, the freezing concrete floors, the drafty windows, the neighbors dressed in rags, the arid brown valley.

I've grown to love my captors.

And I'm also wondering if my love for my captors has turned me crazy when it comes to "going home." Will I go around wielding my philosophical machine guns in normal folks' faces? Will I storm the bank of normalcy and demand Western society to pay up for the good of Africa? In other words, will reverse culture shock zap me?

There's also the other side of this coin. Will my allegiance to Africa make others look at me like I'm the freak? Will the presence of this stranger from Africa cause everyone to feel uncomfortable? Will the mere sight of me be like Patty Hearst wielding a machine gun overhead?

The answers will come soon enough. Eight days, actually. There is one fact that offers me some consolation. Patty Hearst is still alive today. She's out of the SLA, she's out of jail, and she has some semblance of normalcy in her life. Even if I'm feeling like Patty Hearst today, it's good to know that there is life after Patty Hearst—for her and for me.

Epilogue

"The seasons of missions"

Winter: the season to dream

John 12:24
"I tell you the truth, unless a kernel of wheat falls to the ground and dies, it remains only a single seed. But if it dies, it produces many seeds."

Death. Decay. Darkness. The cold, harsh struggle. A lonely landscape. Sacrifice and suffering. Winter.

Years have passed since I've experienced a classic winter in all its stark and brutal drama. Southern California winters were a soap opera actor's blundering farce; Africa winters couldn't even find their way to the stage. But the Northeast, now *there* is a winter. In fact, this current Pennsylvania winter was so desirous of the limelight that it stole a cameo in early fall this year. But now its day has come, and I sit inside this heated room concluding a book on seasons, in the very season of the year that is considered the end of all seasons.

Winter is the hardest time of year. Animals struggle to find food and shelter; some simply sleep away the whole season in hibernation. Plants cannot grow, and the vegetation they had produced has since fallen and decayed, leaving lifeless branches and decapitated stalks to stretch their haunting arms to the sky. Humans mourn the inhospitable climate, cowering indoors from nature's ugly moods. Everyone cherishes the few hours of light, even when the hours don't feature the banished sun. Many thousands suffer seasonal affective disorder, a clinical depression triggered by the long hours of night. Suicide rates are markedly higher in northern regions during the winter. Winter is not our friend.

Yet God has made winter. The writer of Ecclesiastes said, "There is a time for everything, and a season for every activity under heaven" (3:1). Winter has its purpose, both for our planet and for our lives. But what is it? What can be the point of this season of death?

Maybe the story of winter is the story of mankind. Maybe all of human history begins in a kind of winter.

Our God is springtime; He is the creator. "In the beginning, God created,"[1] and the beauty of the galaxies and the sky and the oceans appeared in a joyous explosion of life. Then, living and breathing animals came with their glorious coats and their pulsating muscles. And lastly, He created a creature in His own image, brimming with dynamic intellect, endless creativity, and most of all, the capacity to love. Man and woman were able to live with God for a time in this springtime.

But then something went wrong. Our intellect, creativity, and love made a fatal mistake. We introduced death to God's life. And in this death is where we now live. This death is the background to the Bible, from Genesis 3 all the way to the future day of Revelation 21. But this death is not the end of mankind because our God is not a God of death.

God has worked through history to bring life to a dead people, promising good to Abraham, speaking through Moses, ruling through David, and teaching through the prophets. His desire was that in this world of death there would be a people of life, a people who would call themselves God's very own children. These people would share life with those around them and proclaim an alternative to the winter of mankind. This is the Old Testament story.

But an alternative wasn't enough. God wanted to reintroduce a permanent springtime and to bring mankind back to His beautiful garden. To do this, winter had to be destroyed once-and-for-all. "When the time had fully come, God sent His Son"[2] into the winter, into the death that mankind had created. And here, He did what no man could do—live a perfect life in a

---

[1] Genesis 1:1
[2] Galatians 4:4

dead world and give His perfect life as a ransom for every dead life in the world. Springtime traded places with winter.[3]

Mankind can now immediately choose to have the Spirit of life inside of them thanks to Jesus' sacrifice. They too can be like Christ, men and women of springtime inhabiting a winter world. The New Testament story records the bloom of God's spring. But it also tells the future: mankind's winter will one day end.[4]

I'm far from the first person to use this "winter/spring" metaphor to describe God's plan for rescue and regeneration. C.S. Lewis uses this analogy most famously in *The Lion, the Witch, and the Wardrobe*. The inhabitants of Narnia feel like "it's always winter but never Christmas" before the lion Aslan returns and thaws their frozen world. But when it comes to describing what winter is like in missions, I think a different metaphor is better suited. Let me explain what winter is like for a missionary.

We who believe in the Lord Jesus make it our mission to share eternal life with those near and far. We must go to those living in darkness and proclaim light. There are over 6,600 people groups who have known nothing but winter for their entire histories. Over two and a half billion of the earth's inhabitants have never heard of God's plan of redemption through Jesus Christ.[5] With these statistics in mind, how then can we take this message to those who haven't heard?

Jesus' words in John 12:24 show us the way: through death. We must lay down our own lives, our own preferences, and our own selfish desires in the same way that Jesus lay down His. We must die to ourselves. We must live sacrificially. We

---

[3] 2 Corinthians 5:21 "God made him who had no sin to be sin for us, so that in him we might become the righteousness of God.

[4] Revelation 21-22

[5] All statistics from this chapter are from the Joshua Project. See JoshuaProject.net

must go to those buried in winter and proclaim the resurrection of spring.

Our American culture pushes farther away from this harsh lifestyle. Society's most basic teaching is hedonism. *Live for yourself. If it feels good, do it. Your happiness is what matters most.* Our churches recognize the extreme and destructive ramifications of these sinful notions, yet we find our theology bending to accommodate both the Bible and self-interest. Under our steeples, we set up tiny altars to safety, security, ease, luxury, marriage, friendship, and family. We take these good gifts from God and make them our false gods. Self-interest is put before self-sacrifice.

If we are to be a people of the Great Commission, we need to become like Jesus. Our churches must teach a "whatever-it-takes" attitude towards reaching the unreached. Senders from the West need to live sacrificially and purposefully in a land of affluence. Missionaries must be ready to go boldly into the harshest physical and spiritual places on the planet. Death is necessary to bring life.

Eternal life is the reason we die, for self-sacrifice without a reason is empty. We dream of a day when every people group will have a church. We dream of a day when every person will have heard of Jesus Christ, and many will choose to believe in Him. While winter is a season of death, it's also the season of dreaming what is soon to come.

Those of us involved with missions must live in winter in order to proclaim spring. We must embrace sacrifice, death, desolation, loneliness, pain, and grief in order to proclaim the resurrection of spring. When we die, then our lives will produce many seeds, like the kernel of wheat that dies. We must dream of the beautiful future God has in store for the unreached people groups and know with certainty that many seeds will grow when springtime comes.

Spring: the season to begin

2 Samuel 11:1
In the spring, at the time when kings go off to war, David sent Joab out with the king's men and the whole Israelite army. They destroyed the Ammonites and besieged Rabbah. But David remained in Jerusalem.

After months of winter's lifeless dominion over earth, spring breaks forth with all its beautiful imagery—the fragrance of blossoms, the visual explosion of greens, the comfort of warm breezes, and the sounds of nature rousing from its slumber. As the days lengthen, the dreams and visions from the winter retreat from the realm of fantasy to that of action. Life is ready to begin.

In Bible times, spring was a time of action for nations. Before the herdsmen could take livestock out to graze and farmers could plant their fields, borders needed to be secured. Kings would engage their armies, pushing back any intruders into their territory and taking new lands from anyone whose lines had grown weak. Every good king went to war with his people, on behalf of his people, when springtime came.

One spring, David, generally considered Israel's foremost king, did not go to war. And what would follow this bad decision by a great king was his life's greatest shame. At the very time when he should have been fighting alongside his men, engaging in the activity of spring, he stayed behind and retreated back to winter. He selfishly stole a married woman, conceived an illegitimate child, and murdered the woman's husband. David brought death and destruction to a season of life and new beginnings.

For Christians, for those of us allowing God to build His kingdom through us, today is spring. This is the time for going to our borders and advancing as far as we can with God's Spirit as our sword. This is the time for going to the ends of the world and for sowing seed wherever we can. This is the time to go. Some of you reading this have been sitting on the fence. You've felt God calling you to the mission field, or maybe calling you to partner up via prayer or finances with a missionary. Now is the time to do it. Don't hesitate any longer. Write the letter, send the email, make the call, fill out the application, enroll in the classes, sign the check. Whatever the next step is for you, take it. Today is spring, the season to begin.

I realize that some of my readers find this talk very foreign. You've only ever been taught to be a "missionary" at your school or on the job or in your neighborhood. You've been told to pray for revival in your city but never anywhere else. You're wondering if this emphasis on "going to all nations" is really legitimate.

Acts 1:8 records the resurrected Jesus' words to His disciples: "You will be my witnesses in Jerusalem, and in all Judea and Samaria, and to the ends of the earth." Jerusalem here represents the home culture for his disciples. Therefore, the Bible says we *are* to evangelize our schools and workplaces. We *are* to pray for repentance in our towns. God does care about your "Jerusalem," but this is only one of three target groups Jesus sets before us.

God spends another third of this missions declaration talking about how you should love those who are near you but are slightly different. The people of Samaria had much in common culturally with the people of Judea, but they were outsiders. God tells us to love the outsiders among us as a second target group.

However, His third target group concerns those who are completely and utterly foreign, those hiding in some distant and remote place. He cares about "the ends of the earth" just as much as Jerusalem and Samaria. He loves all of those who are without hope for today and a chance at heaven for eternity, no matter where they live. He instructs us plainly: *I love you, I love your neighbors, I love the outsiders, and I love the ones far off.*

Yet despite His clear commandment here in Acts 1:8 and in Matthew 28:19, we delay, we stay behind, we lag. Not only do we ourselves refuse to go, we're barely sending out others to the mission field. Almost every missionary I know struggles to find and keep financial support. Ninety-nine and one half cent of every American church dollar ministers to Christians; one half penny goes to reaching the unreached. Although there are millions of paid Christian workers crammed between the Atlantic and Pacific Oceans, there are three missionaries—yes, three—for every million unreached Muslims. These pathetic efforts sadly reflect our true attitude towards loving "the ends of the earth" like Jesus does.

We're not going, we're not giving money, and we're not encouraging others to go. This is not fitting behavior for springtime.

Chances are, however, that if you're reading this book, you are involved with missions and are maybe even a missionary yourself. You are already in the battle. You are in the midst of fighting on the front lines or are standing right behind the ranks, supplying them with everything they need. You are, as I'll explain in the next section, more in the summer of your service than in the spring. I commend you for that and praise God for the part you are playing.

But I think there is still a lesson for you from David's spring failure. Never give up. Never stay behind for just a season. Never be satisfied that you've done enough. Never lose focus on why you're giving and sacrificing and suffering for the sake of world missions. The harvest will come. The bounty will soon flood into your life. Rewards are only a blink away in Heaven. Don't miss out because you've grown weary of the fight.

If you feel like leaving the mission field, don't. If you feel like withdrawing your financial support of missions, don't. If you feel like backing down from this calling, don't. If you feel like changing to a higher profile ministry, don't. If you feel like making your family happier by abandoning missions, don't. If you feel like moving your donations to a cause that gives you more immediate gratification, don't. If you feel like doing only what you feel like doing, don't. Don't, don't, don't.

Imagine a spring where the flowers blossom in brown, where the new fruits shrivel on the branch, where the tender shoots retreat into the soil. Imagine a spring where no birds return from the south and no butterflies emerge from their cocoons. Imagine evenings growing dark again and cold breezes returning after just weeks of warmth. God forbid a spring such as this.

Spring isn't the time for withdrawing. Spring is the time for action.

Summer: the season to thrive

Psalm 1:3
He is like a tree planted by streams of water, which yields its fruit in season and whose leaf does not wither. Whatever he does prospers.

The calendar read "July" when we left Africa for our first home assignment. July means rainy season in Kenya, and rainy season usually brings cooler temperatures and soggy terrain. When we stepped off the plane on the East Coast, however, July meant something entirely different. Summer first scalded us with its humidity in the airport parking garage, even at ten o'clock at night.

Our first days back in America didn't just feature heat though. There was rain. Big rain. More rain than we'd had for much of the rainy season in Kenya. And along with the rain and the blistering sun on alternating days, the color green created a lush blanket over the earth. The trees of Pennsylvania—literally "Penn's woods"—coated the horizon in every decoration with thick swaths of forest green. The grass grew faster than you could cut it, and its color was gorgeous to the naked eye, although simply neon in the photos we took of our family at play. And the corn. What can I say about the corn? Beautiful, thick stalks everywhere through this farm country and the height of it was nearly twice what my African neighbors had planted in their *shambas*. I found myself praising God more when I looked at the towering field of maize than any other time, a reflection of how I brought my new African values home with me to America.

Nature thrives in summer. Vegetation thrives, livestock thrives, and the long days allow men and women to work longer and harder than any other time of the year. Nature prospers, but it's not easy for anyone involved. The sheep huddle under pasture trees for shade, the cows wade in the streams, and the horses' tails swish without ceasing as swarms of thriving flies make the heat a double nuisance. And with the flies, the rest of God's creatures—mosquitoes, snakes, ants, and wasps to name a few of my least favorite—all are teeming in summer time. Mankind's toil in summer is doubled too. On top of the increased workload, the heat drains energy, draws out unending perspiration, and mentally wears on us. Summer's success comes at a cost.

In missions, summer time doesn't come right away. It takes time to see your work begin to thrive. You don't simply plop down somewhere and see spiritual fruit. Seasons will need to pass—months for some people and decades for others—before you will have enough cultural wisdom and relational equity with people to see deep transformation and lasting discipleship.

There is a time of dying when you first arrive in a cross-cultural setting, a time when you mourn the familiar life you left behind. During this time, you have nothing. Your emotional and spiritual landscape is barren, desolate, and cold. This is winter.

But all along, like the writer of Psalm 1:3 says, the missionary is planted by the water. God nourishes him, and slowly, the landscape begins to blossom. Relationships are formed, language is decoded, and culture becomes more familiar. The icy chill of homesickness fades a bit, and the small joys of new customs start to bloom. Over time, spring comes for the missionary.

Without the winter and spring, there could never be a summer, and summer is the season of thriving. Summer is when hearts are changed, when eyes are opened, and when souls are saved. But like nature's summer, summer for the missionary isn't easy. To thrive you must first strive to overcome challenges.

What kinds of challenges are in missions today? First and foremost, we face a spiritual challenge. Satan doesn't want to lose ground in his kingdom. And while he will employ a hundred different strategies to subvert a missionary, the final and most decisive action he can execute is martyrdom. More Christians died in the 20th century as martyrs than in the previous nineteen centuries combined. Satan hopes that cutting us down in the height of our effectiveness will spoil the harvest.

The people groups that are still unreached at this point in history are unreached for a reason—their locations are remote and their native climates are inhospitable. The challenges of getting to an isolated mission field and then staying there long enough to see a church planted and the Gospel flourish are great. The missionary soul can wither under this unrelenting strain.

Other unreached people groups are easy to get to, but are ruled by governments opposed to Christianity. While these governments disallow missionaries, they welcome foreign business people who can fuel their economy. Undercover missionaries work all over the world in closed countries, but the heat is always on them. Every conversation about Jesus, every church meeting they conduct, and every prayer that they say could mark the end of their seasons of spiritual progress, or worse, the end of their lives.

Regardless of the type of challenge, however, the toils of summer yield a harvest for the man who remains planted in the Lord. With roots tapping deep into God's abundant joy and peace, he will thrive like a tree planted by streams of water. His fruit will come in the perfect season—just as God desires it—and his leaf will not wither under the challenges of summer.

Whatever he does—Bible translation, technical support, church planting, street evangelism, medical work, aviation, pastoral training, or any other kind of mission—will prosper. Missions thrive in summer.

Fall: the season to rejoice

Matthew 9:37-38
Then he said to his disciples, "The harvest is plentiful but the workers are few. Ask the Lord of the harvest, therefore, to send out workers into his harvest field."

I sometimes fall into the trap all parents fall into. I sometimes think that my children do and say things that are undeniably adorable and indisputably precocious. And like most parents, I share my children's small milestones with anyone who will listen, even though the cute words and actions are far less impressive to anyone outside the circle of mommy and me. Except there is one significant difference between my children and everybody else's: mine actually are the cutest and funniest kids in the world. And since this distinction belongs to me, I'm at liberty to share one last story.

Since we are on home assignment, my son Micah started kindergarten this fall at the local public school in Pennsylvania. A large part of the curriculum centers around the seasons, and since Micah already has a penchant for art, he has embraced decorating our house for each and every holiday that comes our way. Fall is the time of beautiful colors and plentiful crops, so our walls and fridge have been filled with cutouts of leaves and pumpkins, and pictures of apple trees and cornfields.

In fact, his love for each season and each holiday is so extreme that he was horrified when he went to his aunt and uncle's house right after Halloween. They started pulling out Christmas decorations in mid-November, and Micah was near tears. His pain continued in the department stores and malls; Christmas decorations were everywhere. Crestfallen, he sunk his head into his mother's side and lamented like a five-year-old Martha Stewart, "Why doesn't anyone decorate for Thanksgiving?"

Fall is the season of harvest, and Thanksgiving the American holiday to celebrate abundance in our lives. The earth is finished with its work, having borne all the fruit and vegetables it can. The farmers have toiled and labored through the spring and summer, with the reward of full barns, full silos, and full pantries realized in fall. The culmination of all things has come; nature gives its final encore in a blush of brilliant reds, oranges, and yellows. As we've driven around the region speaking about missions and visiting with relatives, I can't count how many times God took my breath away with the beauty of fall.

Earlier, I used spring as an analogy for the new birth that happens in a believer's life and how Jesus banished winter forever with His death and resurrection. However, Jesus chose another seasonal metaphor when He described His way of looking at the world. Jesus says it's harvest time.

"I tell you, open your eyes and look at the fields! They are ripe for harvest. Even now the reaper draws his wages, even now he harvests the crop for eternal life, so that the sower and the reaper may be glad together. Thus the saying 'One sows and another reaps' is true. I sent you to reap what you have not worked for. Others have done the hard work, and you have reaped the benefit of their labor" (John 4:35b-38).

Jesus tells us that now is the time to rejoice. He Himself has done all of the critical work—taking each and every sin of mine and yours and of the whole world—and now *we* get to enjoy the harvest. The harvest itself does indeed take some effort on our part—that's what worldwide missions are about—but the fruit of our labor is so tangible and so imminent that Christ says we are "drawing our wages" and are "glad" and have "reaped the benefit" even while we work.

Sometimes we are tricked into misunderstanding what Jesus meant when He talked about harvest. Somehow we envision ourselves laboring in His field, bringing in His crop, and then being locked out in the cold in some dilapidated shed with nothing to eat. But that's not what happens at harvest time. In God's harvest time, He sits us down to a savory feast *today* and promises us a double-portion *tomorrow*. When you compare our miniscule work and our microscopic sacrifice with Christ's work and sacrifice, it's like placing a seed next to all the cornfields in Nebraska. Our blessings truly are far greater than our labors.

Missionaries are the luckiest people of earth. We get to see firsthand the incredible Spirit of God first transform individuals who had never heard of Jesus before and then revolutionize entire communities. We are the specially chosen and specially blessed ones who are sent out by hundreds of other believers to work in God's fields. We live in a place of harvest.

Supporters of missionaries are the luckiest people on earth too. You get to be in two places at once, as you serve and love people in Jesus' name at home while praying and giving for people abroad whom you'll never meet. You are the impassioned visionaries with a calling to send out countless missionaries into numerous fields to bring home the harvest for God's glory, even while you taste a harvest here in your own backyard.

Seasons. Winter, spring, summer, and fall. Rainy season and dry season. Whatever we call them, there is no denying that each season of life holds its own charm and its own blessings. Ecclesiastes 3:11 says, "He has made everything beautiful in its time." Each season of the missionary life—Winter, the time to dream; Spring, the time to begin; Summer, the time to thrive; and Fall, the time to rejoice. Each season is beautiful; each season works together to a crescendo of God's glory shouted by "every nation, tribe, people, and language" (Revelation 7:9).

And when that final day comes, we'll rejoice at how the Lord of the harvest answered our feverish prayers to send more workers. And we'll marvel at how we lasted all those years in missions, and we'll each tell stories of God's grace and mercy through the seasons of sacrificing and giving.

Heaven's walls will be decorated with the works of God's children. And our loving Father will say the words we long to hear from Him.

Well done.